The Culture of
Religious Pluralism

Explorations:
Contemporary Perspectives on Religion

*Lynn Davidman, Gillian Lindt, Charles H. Long, John P. Reeder Jr.,
Ninian Smart, John F. Wilson, and Robert Wuthnow, Advisory Board*

The Culture
of Religious
Pluralism

Richard E. Wentz
Arizona State University

📖 WestviewPress
A Division of HarperCollinsPublishers

Explorations: Contemporary Perspectives on Religion

Copyright © 1998 by Westview Press, A Division of HarperCollins Publishers, Inc.

Published in 1998 in the United States of America by Westview Press, 5500 Central Avenue, Boulder, Colorado 80301-2877, and in the United Kingdom by Westview Press, 12 Hid's Copse Road, Cumnor Hill, Oxford OX2 9JJ

A CIP catalog record for this book is available from the Library of Congress.
ISBN 0-8133-2643-5 (hc) — ISBN 0-8133-2644-3 (pb)

The paper used in this publication meets the requirements of the American National Standard for Permanence of Paper for Printed Library Materials Z39.48-1984.

10   9   8   7   6   5   4   3   2   1

For Cynthia

. . . all he did was spread the room
Of our enacting out the doom
Of being in each other's way,
And so put off the weary day
When we would have to put our mind
On how to crowd but still be kind.

"America Is Hard to See"
—Robert Frost

Pluralism means, then, not only the division into many
different ecclesiastical organizations and theological points of
view, but also a state of mind instinctively defensive of it.

"The Fact of Pluralism and
the Persistence of Sectarianism"
—Sidney E. Mead

This book is dedicated to Sidney E. Mead (1904–), good friend of these latter days, who set before me the task herein.

My study of religion in American history, whatever else it
may be, becomes a quest to discover and delineate the religion
of the pluralistic culture in which I have lived and moved and
had my being.

"In Quest of America's Religion"
—Sidney E. Mead

Contents

Preface

This book emerges out of a conversation with Spencer Carr, at the time a senior editor with Westview Press. The project grew out of his suggestion that I have a "go" at the business of describing the contours of pluralism. Because my scholarly career has been spent thinking about religion in American history, I have quite naturally explored pluralism in that context.

I owe a great deal to so many people whose ideas have become part of my own language. I cannot give them all credit, for fear of leaving out the names of dear friends and others who contributed, often unknowingly, to my hermeneutical maneuvers. However, I have singled out Sidney Mead for my dedication because I am very much in harmony with his imaginative handling of "data" referred to as "history," and also because I have come to know him so well since he came to Arizona to live out his latter days. Although "trained" as a historian, I have been most interested in what history means, with how we may use historical perspective to create a meaningful discourse about human destiny.

As usual, my wife, Cynthia, has provided the critical nudging that challenges cherished ideas. She is a scholar of considerable scope, and one devoted to issues of religion and justice, particularly with regard to Native Americans. She keeps me as honest as possible to the degree that I allow anyone to tamper with the dishonesty that resides within. She will recognize many of her own ideas within these pages.

To all those who may somehow learn that human religiousness is greater than the sum of religions, I offer this study. We cannot proceed, however, without friendly acknowledgment of the faithfulness of Jim Dybdahl, who has worked with my handwritten manuscripts for many years, transforming them into documents suitable for editorial action.

Richard E. Wentz

1
Diversity and Pluralism: An Introduction

A culture can be defined as an identifiable and regularized behavior that is attributable to a particular people and that is expressed through certain images, symbols, rituals, myths, and other kinds of stories. Art, music, literature, celebrations, and other distinctive creations and behaviors are all cultural forms; they give expression to the manner in which a certain people in their time and place live out their days. Cultures do not die; they undergo constant transformation. A culture that is believed to be "dead" usually lives on among a people who have memories of a mythic and legendary past. Even the "dead" language of a culture may live in words, symbols, and stories that continue to be important. It was long thought that the pre-Columbian cultures of Mexico and Central and South America were extinct. However, we are increasingly aware of the fact that the Incan and Aztec cultures live on among peoples whose present circumstances still reflect their cultural ancestry.

Culture is a difficult subject for academic study; it is inventive, changing, and elusive. Cultural study becomes a kind of mural painting, an affair of constantly identifying new elements and extending the tapestry. Therefore, cultural study is an interesting, even a fascinating intellectual enterprise. As Franklin Gamwell reminds us: "[The word] 'religion' is frequently used, at least in the first instance, to identify a form of culture."[1] This would imply, of course, that religion and culture are virtually indistinguishable terms. It would mean that what we call "religions" are those identifiable cultural forms associated with distinctive ways of living. Although religion and culture are finally indistinguishable, it is useful to understand that religion represents a particular reading of culture. Religion concerns itself with the manner in which cultural forms express a certain sense of the ultimate order and meaning of existence. The study of religion is therefore never satisfied with the definitions and proscriptions provided by official councils and their doctrines. It must take an academic reading of the entire culture. As Sam Gill puts it in his study of the religions of nonliterate peoples:

We are faced with great opportunities and challenges in the study of nonliterate peoples. The opportunities rest upon extending our knowledge of religious belief and practice in the cultural domains where religion is lived by all the people of a culture, a dimension to which in nonliterate cultures we are nearly confined. This cultural dimension exists in religions everywhere, but it has been largely ignored by religion scholars because of a preference to study religion in terms of its written documents. We are presented with the challenge to learn how to read and to understand the religious significance of elements of expression that are not written, such things as art, architecture, oral traditions, and ritual.[2]

The culture of America is measured to a great extent by its diversity. American art, architecture, music, and oral traditions have been shaped by diversity and by the need to accommodate the desire for unity to the necessity of accepting "manyness." The mutual encounters of Europeans, Native Americans, and Africans have fashioned a culture in which the religious need to give expression to ultimate order and meaning must take constant account of diversity. In America there are not only many religions; there is a religiousness that arises from the circumstances of that manyness. In other words, even if Americans live within their own religious particularities, when they accept manyness they acknowledge some perception of order and meaning not confined to their traditional religious loyalties.

The culture of religious pluralism is ever changing as new religious and ethnic groups arrive upon the scene, and also as our religiousness breaks out of its existing forms and joins in the many struggles for order and meaning in the midst of chaos. European religious consciousness in the North American context emerged out of the cultural revolution known as the Reformation of the sixteenth century. This was a chaotic struggle among diverse claims to authentic Christianity. Even the colonialism that accompanied the Reformation was more than a matter of economic or political manipulation. Geographic and demographic horizons were being radically shifted, and the questions of ultimate truth and salvation were directed toward mastering those who threatened existing perceptions of reality. The diversity generated in the sixteenth century, and exported to the New World almost immediately, has been a constant factor in American religious and cultural life.

The story of America is the story of this diversity and the hope of transcending its fragmentary effects. The thesis of this book is that the transformation of diversity into pluralism is a religious phenomenon that serves as a prevailing factor in the development of American culture. Pluralism denotes the acceptance of diversity; and this acceptance, we have observed, always works within some perception of ultimate order and meaning not confined to traditional religions.[3]

This, I take it, is what Sidney Mead means when, in the two essays cited on the dedication page of this book, he points to pluralism as a state of mind supportive of diversity and to his own quest to discern "the religion of the pluralistic culture in which [he has] lived and moved and had [his] being."[4] The usual academic distinction between the descriptive and the normative does not hold as we contemplate Mead's ideas and the thesis I have set forth. Certainly this enterprise will reveal the depth of my commitment to the descriptive mode. I wish to set clearly before the reader the contours of American religious diversity and the manner in which each stage of American history has revealed the religious need to find a pluralistic posture of acceptance. But the attempt to understand the process of transformation cannot be only a matter of description. For, as Mead has pointed out: "[The] study of the history of the religion of one's culture is perhaps the most direct and efficacious route to self-understanding, and that insofar as the historian is immersed in his culture (as I am in mine) his history of the religion of his culture is his 'internal' history and his approach will be 'autobiographical.'"[5] For Mead, the task of interpreting *traditional* or particular religions will likely be biographical rather than autobiographical. There is a certain sense of "outsiderness" that one accepts by admitting that one cannot live the lives of all people being studied. One becomes an empathetic biographer. However, all are common residents in a diverse culture where autobiographical assumptions are at work; it is not easy to separate oneself from the larger culture, and therefore the pursuit of understanding the religious dimension of pluralistic America is to some extent an exercise in self-understanding. "The American experience," says Mead, ". . . has undermined real belief in the ultimacy of sectarian possibilities."[6] It has done so by reminding the devotees of each tradition that they are not God. That reminder is an essential element in the religious mind that learns to transform the particularisms of diversity into pluralism. To discover the truth of this statement is to move beyond mere functional description. It is a mode of self-understanding fashioned in the autobiographical necessities of a culture in which I am not an outsider.

I cannot escape those questions that are concerned with living together meaningfully in a common culture, even though I commit myself to the description of what I observe in the history of American religion and culture. Traditional societies, whether Native American, European Christian, or African, developed their cultures on the assumption that social order depended upon commonly shared rituals, symbols, and myths.[7] These societies also assumed that their traditions had to be maintained by responsible and continuous leadership (e.g., by priests, storytellers, or medicine men, all of whom have their counterparts in modern societies). The natural diversity of human societies was disrupted by the emergence of modern ideas and technologies, beginning in the sixteenth century. Modern diversity (which is the only kind that the United States has known) is characterized by rapid and dramatic encounters that thrust people together in sacred spaces that had traditionally been occupied only by people with common worldviews. In the modern era, which encompasses America's history from colonial times to the present, religious and cultural diversity could not exist either in parallel or shared sacred space. Diversity tended to exist *within* a broadly shared geographical area. As a result, the people occupying American space found it difficult to agree on shared rituals, symbols, and myths, and even more difficult to establish any appropriate leadership or authority for the maintenance of a common tradition.

The Meaning of Pluralism

Before launching into a discussion of the many forms of America's religious and cultural diversity, I wish to explore some theoretical implications of the concept of pluralism. Because this is *American* history we are trying to understand, the American reader will have more than an academic interest in the subject. Diversity becomes pluralism because Americans all belong to their nation together, some as members of traditions or with commitments to specific religions, others without such relationships. Some Americans may not even feel any particular attachment to the nation itself. But the fact remains that, unless Americans wish to force their individual sentiments and motivations on the rest of society, they must all think together about the meaning of their country's diversity.

Sooner or later, someone will challenge our ideas and loyalties. We may begin to wonder whether our loyalties are "true." The question of the "truth" of what we think probably only arises when we become aware of "others" who think and act differently. They may ask us why we think and act as we do; or we may suddenly begin asking these questions of ourselves. The question of truth is a question of the reliability of our ideas and assumptions. Can I rely on what *I* think in the face of those who apparently think differently? Is what I think *true?* Does it measure up to the size of the world we occupy? The question of truth asks: How far outward does what I think extend? How far do my convictions go and how do they stack up against other ideas, of which I am only beginning to be aware?

Of course, our question is also important because our loyalties have to do with power. Sometimes we are told that power is a bad thing. However, power is an enabler. It is the resource that makes it possible for human beings to contribute to and maintain their own well-being and the well-being of those who belong to their circle of responsibility and concern. We need power to exist meaningfully and without undue dependence upon others who may threaten our well-being. Power is important, and the use of power is a delicate enterprise. Our loyalties empower us; they set conditions and provide resources for the conduct of our lives. In a world where there is but *one* form of loyalty, there are likely to be few limitations on the use of the power generated by that loyalty. As different loyalties increase in *number*, however, the people who represent each set of loyalties will experience various adjustments and curtailments of power.

Diversity *within* commonly shared political and economic space raises questions of more than loyalty and power. One of the most difficult of the issues before us is the matter of identity. Who am I? Who are we? I may assume that my identity is bound up with religious assumptions (including atheism and secularism) that are ethnic, ecclesiastical, or intellectual. That is to say, I may find it meaningful to identify myself as Polish Catholic, Orthodox Jewish, Irish Catholic, Swedish Lutheran, or Southern Baptist. However, it is difficult to nurture that identity in a space that is shared with others whose identity is different. That is why so many of our cherished commitments remain private; why, indeed, we consider discussion of religion and politics to be taboo in social settings. I am an American, and I live among people whose very presence challenges the public validity of my identity. How can I reconcile being Navajo and American at the same time? How can I be Jewish and American, Roman Catholic and American? Does one identity cancel another out?

These issues of power, loyalty, and identity are religious because they have to do with ultimate order and meaning. These are the issues that begin to fashion "the religion of the pluralistic culture" of which Mead speaks; they create pluralism because they affirm a set of values beyond our traditional allegiances. Diversity becomes pluralism, creating symbols, ideas, rituals, and myths that maintain the worth of plurality. Pluralism becomes a religious phenomenon, and a study of the culture of religious pluralism becomes more than an enterprise in the social sciences. American culture is based upon the religious assumptions of pluralism and encompasses the relationship of traditional religions to the religion of pluralism.

The Study of Religion

Religious studies is a relatively new academic discipline, and the communities of higher education are still surprisingly ignorant of the nature of the enterprise. One of the characteristics of the modern world has been the differentiation of the fullness of human activity into separate and compartmentalized units that are thought of as distinct and readily definable. Scholars who live in this kind of compartmentalized world assume that they can satisfactorily define these separate activities. One problem that emerges from such an assumption is that the scholar tends to believe that these limited definitions are objectively real. Accordingly, anthropologists, sociologists, and psychologists may define religion conveniently in keeping with their own compartmentalized notions and not realize the superficiality of their work.

Religious studies scholars attempt to gain as comprehensive a view of human thought and action as possible. These scholars are not satisfied with examining only what the social sciences call "religion." Instead, they find religiousness expressed in almost all human endeavor. They move behind, before, and beyond, as well as into, the compartments called "religion" in order to encounter those ideas, images, and actions that express the ultimate order and meaning of existence for a people in a certain time and place. Accordingly, we can understand how and why the rest of the academic world may have no notion of what the discipline of religious studies is. Many may inexcusably assume that the enterprise is a specifically religious (in the sense of "pious" or "devout") field of study. Yet what are called "religious commitments" or "experiences" are neither here nor there in the opinions of religious studies scholars; they are simply part of what is to be examined.

Scholars are concerned with religious ideas, images, and actions regardless of the context in which they may occur—whether that be religion or politics. They examine religious beliefs, commitments, and devotion as part of a comprehensive enterprise of trying to understand how humans express notions of ultimate order and meaning.

There are three modes in which religiousness is expressed: the verbal, the practical, and the social or communal.[8] The verbal expression of religiousness has to do with the work of intelligence, the mind, and the use of words (hence verbal). We must remember, of course, that human intelligence is to some extent dependent upon the time and circumstances under consideration. An inhabitant of a remote Amazon wilderness is possessed of an intelligence that is different from that of twentieth-century Americans, but it is not to be considered inferior. The verbal expression of our religiousness has to do with ideas, images, intuitions, and convictions discerned by our minds as we respond to our status as human beings in an existence that seems greater than the sum of its parts. We derive ideas of gods or God, of first cause or primal force. Our minds formulate theories like Henri Bergson's *elan vital* that provide a sense of ultimate order and meaning, helping us to understand life. The people of the Hopi mesas of north central Arizona speak of kachinas as spirit beings inhabiting the San Francisco peaks and visiting the mesas to animate the seasons and the cycles of fertility and growth. These too are ideas and images, relying upon language (words) that is shared by people to express the ultimate order and meaning of things. Whether we speak of beliefs, convictions, ideas, doctrines, or revelations, we allude to the propensity of the mind to discern, to think, and to communicate that which is necessary for an ordered and meaningful life.

The mind works with symbols and images that are formed by our social intelligence and imagination. They are part of the verbal mode of religiousness. The practical expression of these symbols has to do with actions and practices, with things done. We must not make the mistake of thinking that the practical mode *follows* or acts out what is *first* thought or believed. I recently came across this erroneous assumption in a book by Rollo May, the distinguished psychotherapist. In *The Cry for Myth*, May tells us that rituals act out and dramatize myths.[9] This may or may not be the case. But the point is that human beings often ritualize their response to what it means to be human without first fashioning a story or a set of ideas or beliefs about their world. Contemplation, storytelling, or the development of doctrine may come *after* performative response to existence has been established.

Imagine, for example, the ancient peoples who lived in or near the deserts and other arid regions of the world. When the rains came, these people were like the birds who danced and chirped. They danced like the raindrops, laughing and crying at the same time, chattering and mimicking the rain and the birds.

Soon they remembered what they had done, and whenever the rains came they performed in the same way. But at first they remembered by doing, not by thinking. The thinking came later; and in this thinking there was a close association between the coming of the rains and their own spontaneous response. Soon there were stories of how the powerful spirits came down from the mountains, gathered in the clouds, and danced their way into the deserts, taking the hands of the people and lifting their faces in gratitude. The performance became an essential part of life. Without the performance there was no rain and no food. The performance was a ritual practice that belonged to the people and expressed the ultimate order and meaning of their existence. We might even say that the ritual action was a mode of "thinking."

But what was perhaps more important than anything else was that the desert planters were a people. Belonging to each other and then to the world about them was itself the most profound expression of ultimate order and meaning. Belonging and the identity that is integral to belonging are highly imaginative realities that fashion human existence. When the Navajo say "We are Dinéh," they are in fact making a statement about what is most real to them. They are *the* people; belonging to *the people* is a most sacred trust. Life assumes order and meaning because they are of the world. They are the people who live in this place, tell these stories, and order their lives with ritual and visions and rules guiding daily behavior.

The people are a sacred people, a sacred reality; their world is a sacred place. Now, I would suggest that these characteristics are also true of people who are not "traditional" people like the Navajo. For some people, to be able to say "I am an American" is sufficient. These kinds of Americans live with the assumption that life makes sense, that life is "together" for them because they are American. They need no other loyalty. Americans share certain ideas, values, and convictions; they celebrate certain special days and consult certain "sacred writings" like the Declaration of Independence, the Constitution, and Lincoln's Gettysburg Address. They do this because they belong, because life as an American is sacred.

This communal or social mode of religious expression, I suggest, is the most significant of the three. For example, there are indications that people in our age are drawn to religious movements like the Church of Jesus Christ of Latter-day Saints (the Mormon church) because such groups offer a true sense of community. As a result, members know who they are and to whom they belong. They are able to say, "We are Latter-day Saints." *Because* the communal is the primary fact of their existence, they are then able to learn the Mormon story and read of their own origins in the Book of Mormon. They are then also able to participate in the ordinances and endowments and other practices that are part of the sacred life of the Mormon people.

Millenarian Christians, like the Seventh-Day Adventists and Jehovah's Witnesses, trace their origins to nineteenth-century Americans like William Miller, who sought to decipher the symbolism of The Revelation to John so as to calculate the date of the second coming of Christ. Presumably these kinds of calculations and predictions became part of the verbal mode of religious expression of the people who followed Miller. They would seem to be core beliefs or ideas. Now, if these ideas represented the *primary* mode of religious expression, we might expect to learn of large-scale defections from the movement when the calculations proved inaccurate, when the ideas or beliefs "failed." Yet the membership tended to remain loyal. Even in recent times, these millenarian groups have maintained a consistent membership (and even grown) through many phases of new calculations and reinterpretations. This suggests that the communal mode of religious expression is primary. Belonging to a unique community of ultimate order and meaning often gives sanction to the special stories, ideas, and experiences shared by that community.

This insight into the significance of the communal mode of religious expression is very important to the understanding of religious pluralism. Identity, power, and loyalty are aspects of all three modes of religious expression, but they are most strongly associated with the social or communal mode. The ultimate order and meaning of existence are expressed in "peoplehood"; identity is knowing to whom we belong, to what people.

But in a complex modern world there are great numbers of people who share the same space. Our identity is constantly measured and shaped by proximity to others who constitute society's diversity. Identity in such a situation as this is precarious indeed, unless, of course, we may begin to understand that the sociality that expresses ultimate order and meaning in the context of our particular people is not exhausted by that context. Perhaps identity is more than what is revealed in our particular tradition; perhaps it is more than the sum of the identities expressed in the diversity of peoples. These are some of the considerations that lead to a transformation of diversity into pluralism.

From Diversity to Pluralism

When Christianity came to life among a small group of Jews in the eastern Mediterranean at the dawn of the Common Era (C.E.), many early devotees of Christ were at first satisfied to remain Jewish. There was no threat to the inherited communal mode of religious expression. Gradually, however, certain ideas and practices began to set them apart from "other" Jews. Eventually they were no longer Jews, but Christ-people; and as they circulated along the caravan routes and military roads of the Roman Empire they found themselves adrift in an ocean of "others"—a world of manyness, many religious groups that provided members with the communal mode of religious expression. There were Mithraists and Zoroastrians, the Bacchi and the worshippers of Osiris and Isis. There were those who worshipped Caesar. The Christians made their way among these diverse groups and tried to figure out who they themselves were in the phantasmagoria. At first the followers of Christ were not concerned with "being Christian," only with sharing the meaning of the life, death, and resurrection of Jesus the Christ of the Jews, then of the Gentiles. It was a proclamation addressed to the diversity of religious traditions. As the Greek philosopher Celsus put it near the end of the second century, "There is nothing wrong if each people observes its own laws of worship. Actually we find that the difference between each nation is very considerable and nevertheless each one of them appears to think its own the best." Each thought its own system the best because it was linked to a particular city or nation—really to *a people*. Therefore, this ancient resolution of religious diversity was to "live and let live." The "laws of worship" were like skin color, dress, dialect, or manners associated with ethnic or national identity. But the Christians were no longer ethnic or national. They began to include people from varied nationalities and ethnic backgrounds. Their advent broke the bonds between religion and specific nations or peoples. Their presence called for a different resolution of diversity. They thought to transcend it. However, the circumstances of history would eventually transform Christianity into a competing element among other systems of belief. They would become one more religion, contributing to diversity and trying to justify the uniqueness, even the superiority, of their claims. This struggle to justify distinctiveness amid diversity rather than to settle for the broader truth of pluralism led to greater diversity, as different teachers and groups sought to separate themselves from those whom they considered false representatives of Christian teaching.

By the fourth century, the theories concerning the nature of Christ, the Trinity, and the Church as the universal embodiment of salvation of the world had all been worked out. The Roman Empire and the Church were ready for the changes wrought by the Emperors Constantine and Theodosius: Christianity was to become the established order of the Empire. Christianity became a religion in the ancient sense of worship that is linked to a particular people, city, or nation (in this case, an empire). Christianity became a religion in the manner in which most people were prepared to think of religion. The problem of diversity was theoretically solved by assigning the status of "outsider" to all other "ways" of worship.

For western Europe, at least, the next twelve centuries were a time of carefully regulated diversity. The authority of the Roman Catholic Church hovered like a giant parasol shading the variety of religious practices that continued alongside of and within the life of Christianity. There were the many ancient traditions of druids and Celts—the ways of the folk. These varieties of pagan ritual practices and healing arts existed under the watchful eyes of Christian princes and priests. Even within the Church's own careful structure, Benedictines and Franciscans, Meister Eckhart, and the Brethren of the Common Life represented examples of the diversity of interpretations of teaching and practice.

In the fourteenth and fifteenth centuries there were signs that diversity of opinion and practice was leading to varied degrees of conflict, even to schism and separation. In England the work of John Wycliffe and the Lollards had begun to erode the stability of the Roman Catholic pluralistic settlement. In Bohemia the followers of John Huss had sown the seeds of dissent that were later to blossom in the protests of Martin Luther, Ulrich Zwingli, and John Calvin. What is called "the Reformation" of the sixteenth century was an explosion of the diversity that had long been present in Western Christianity. The Roman order was fragmented and splintered. Something new was occurring in the history of religion. A religion that had assumed worldwide proportions was faced with a plurality of claims to its own teachings and practices. From the sixteenth century onward there were to be many Christianities (one should say, many more Christianities than there had been before) in the world.

Nevertheless, this diversity was the result of competing claims to the truth of an existing tradition. The diversity was a form of sectarianism resulting from diverse claims to the same basic truth—in this case the truth about the relation of Jesus Christ to human destiny. It is important to understand that this diversity within Christian tradition has been the primary form of diversity acknowledged by most Americans until well into the twentieth century. Pluralism had not yet become a religious resolution to the problems posed by diversity.

The Reformation occurred just as the Western Hemisphere was opened to exploration and settlement. Spain sent its conquistadors into what was to become Mexico and the American Southwest accompanied by priests and missionaries of the Society of Jesus, a religious order formed to counter the effects of the Protestant side of the Reformation. When the English began to colonize America's eastern seaboard, they opened the lands along the Atlantic coast to numerous offspring of the English and continental Reformations. In a sense, the thirteen colonies that made up the original United States were home to a wide-ranging Protestant diversity. There were the several varieties of Puritanism that emerged out of the Church of England. There were Anglicans, Presbyterians, Congregationalists, and Quakers. From the continent there arrived Swedish and German Lutherans, Dutch Reformed, Mennonites, and a considerable array of small sectarian and cultic groups. Of course, Roman Catholics and Jews also came, but they were a small minority at first. "Protestant" diversity was without a doubt the dominant religious configuration in the United States from the colonial period well into the nineteenth century. Whatever religious conflicts emerged were intramural, played out within the scope of Protestant Christian diversity.

The first real hints of a disturbance of the Protestant status quo occurred in the 1830s and 1840s. The story of mass immigration begins during this time with the flight of German Jews and Irish Catholics seeking refuge in large numbers from oppression, social change, and famine. From the colonial period to the early nineteenth century, emigration from Europe and Britain was slow and took place in small numbers. But by the 1830s the new American republic had become the setting for the dramatic technological, industrial, and social changes that measured the progressing history of the late modern world.

Many representatives of the Protestant cultural "establishment" feared the collapse of their world, the erosion of their values, and the threat to the truth of their salvation posed by the religious pretenses of the Antichrist and Satan. In their own minds they became "natives," defending their families and their country against the alien invaders of the Promised Land. Catholics and (interestingly enough) to a lesser extent, Jews, were false pretenders to the truth offered by the God of Abraham,

Isaac, Jacob, and Jesus. A certain amount of violence was perpetrated in the name of religion. The anti-Catholic propaganda of the "nativists" maintained in discordant variations the same themes composed in the heat of the sixteenth-century Reformation. Much of this sentiment continued to some degree well into the twentieth century (perhaps until the election of the Catholic John F. Kennedy to the presidency). But after the initial enthusiasm the credibility of anti-Catholic propaganda gradually ebbed. American society required a more creative adjustment to religious, cultural, and ethnic diversity.

The German Jews who immigrated in the nineteenth century sought to minimize their presence by adopting the outward styles of Protestantism. Rabbis and synagogues became modern, outwardly emulating the Protestant world around them. The Roman Catholics, however, did not so easily settle into the Protestant Christian world of that century. They objected to the use of the King James Version of the Bible in the emerging public schools, regarding it as a "Protestant" document that taught values inimical to Catholic truth. They saw the public schools as the institutions of a Protestant establishment. When their efforts to forestall the introduction of the King James Bible into the school system failed, they began the arduous task of fashioning a parochial educational system, a monumental accomplishment nowhere duplicated in the modern world. Parochial schools are a memorial of the Catholic response to the established order of Protestant diversity.

However, there were many American Roman Catholics, like Orestes Brownson, Isaac Hecker, and James Cardinal Gibbons, who sought to interpret Catholic truth as being compatible with the American republic. Eventually, their wrists were lightly slapped by the Vatican because European and American Catholic traditionalists were fearful that the "Americanization" of the Catholic Church was a basic threat to the authority of Rome. But new ideas can eventually have their way with us: They can be condemned, but they do not readily disappear. Instead, they make their way subtly into our thinking, often influencing even those who consciously oppose them.

Roman Catholics gradually adjusted to the Protestant world. Everyone has heard one of the countless jokes about the priest, the minister, and the rabbi, often cavorting together on the golf course, teasing each other about their differences. These jokes are an important part of American folklore, demonstrating a quality of cultural diversity in which people are different, yet know how to get along congenially. Catholics and Protestants began to see themselves as part of a shared Christian world in which they could accommodate each other, even though theologians of one or the other "tradition" interpreted their respective traditions to be the "one, true Church" or representative of the "true Christian faith." By the mid-twentieth century Protestant Christian diversity had been transformed into a broader "Christian" diversity that included Roman Catholics. The mandate for pluralism was not far away.

Interestingly enough, the word "Christian" underwent a transformation of meaning in some quarters. For many Americans, including educators like Charles Franklin Thwing, president of the University of Michigan and a popular writer on education, a "Christian" came to mean a "monotheist"—one who affirmed faith in the God of the Bible, the God of Abraham, Isaac, Jacob, and Jesus. This meant, in effect, that "Christian" was in some way inclusive of "Jew," an assumption perhaps demonstrably less acceptable to traditional Jews than to liberal Christian monotheists.

By 1955, the Jewish sociologist of religion, Will Herberg, had published what has become a classic of twentieth-century academic literature. In _Protestant, Catholic, and Jew_, Herberg claimed that Americans identified themselves, _as Americans_, as belonging to one of three traditions. The American Way could be Protestant, Catholic, or Jewish. For Herberg, American religious life was in reality a trinity. _E pluribus unum_ meant that there was a religious unity to America, a unity that was three-in-one, three personae in one essence. The ink was hardly dry in this very important book before it became evident that America's diversity was much more radical than Herberg's trinitarian formula made it out to be.

The radicalism of religious diversity is a fact of contemporary life and may well become the most significant feature in the development of society and culture in the twenty-first century. This diversity is radical because it expresses the very rootedness (radix) of our shared humanity on the planet. Since the passage of the Immigration Act of 1965, America's diversity has broken out of its sectarian Christian rivalries and Biblical toleration to include Buddhists, Muslims, Hindus, and others from many parts of the globe. Although some representatives of these traditions may assume very sectarian postures, they must share the American space.

A Muslim living in the United States today is not a Muslim only when he visits the mosque, recites _Allah akbar_, or fasts during the sacred month of Ramadan. He is a Muslim when he votes in a local election, goes to market, visits a museum, or reads the newspaper. He is, indeed, a Muslim when he meets a Christian or a Jew in the local park. "To each among you [the various communities of mankind]," says the Qur'an, "we have prescribed a Law and an Open Way. If God had so willed, He would have made you a single people, but [His plan is] to test you in what He hath given you: so strive as in a race in all virtues. The goal of you all is to God; it is He that will show you the truth of the matters in which ye dispute" (Holy Qur'an, 5:48).

Apparently, classical Islam sought to recognize the positive virtues of diversity, assuming only that each "Law" and "Way" would lead to the affirmation of "One God" and a "Day of Judgment" (ultimate moral responsibility). This Qur'anic insight is suggestive of the new direction of America's religious and cultural diversity. Whether pluralism is able to accommodate the religious needs of the new society remains to be seen. Perhaps pluralism's religious significance must first be recognized so that Americans can defend the richness of their new diversity, recognizing with Sidney Mead that "the American experience . . . has undermined real belief in the ultimacy of sectarian possibilities," reminding sectarian devotees that they are not God and that "it is He that will show you the truth of the matters in which ye dispute." If pluralism is to become a mainstay of American culture, then Americans must all share its understanding that the goodness of life requires them to accept life as greater than the sum of individual knowledge and commitments.

Notes

1. Franklin I. Gamwell, *The Meaning of Religious Freedom* (Albany: State University of New York Press, 1995), p. 22.

2. Sam D. Gill, *Beyond "the Primitive": The Religions of Nonliterate Peoples* (Englewood Cliffs, NJ: Prentice-Hall, 1982), pp. 111–112.

3. Gamwell, pp. 22, 77–78.

4. Sidney E. Mead, "The Fact of Pluralism and the Persistence of Sectarianism," and "In Quest of America's Religion," *The Nation with the Soul of a Church* (New York: Harper & Row, 1975), pp. 4, 5, 38.

5. Mead, p. 4.

6. Mead, p. 9.

7. Cf. Peter Berger, *The Sacred Canopy* (New York: Doubleday, 1967), esp. pt. 1.

8. See Joachim Wach, *The Comparative Study of Religion* (New York: Columbia University Press, 1958); or Richard E. Wentz, *Religion in the New World: The Shaping of Religious Traditions in the United States* (Minneapolis: Fortress Press, 1990), chap. 1.

9. Rollo May, *The Cry for Myth* (New York: W. W. Norton & Company, 1991), p. 290.

2

Conquest and Conversion: Models of Response to Diversity

Diversity is the awareness of manyness, the discovery that there are "others" besides us and our own communities. Diversity is a recognition of the dynamic "otherness" of existence. "Modern man," wrote Loren Eiseley, "who has not contemplated his otherness, the multiplicity of other possible people who dwell or might have dwelt in him, has not realized the full terror and responsibility of existence."[1] The failure to contemplate this otherness is not an exclusively modern predicament. It seems that human societies have always had great difficulty owning up to "the multiplicity of other possible people who dwell or might have dwelt in [us]." The circumstances of modernity have exacerbated this condition by increasing the intensity and rapidity of our encounters with others. And, in these circumstances, individuals and groups often tend to think of themselves as isolated and private entities. Diversity represents a threat to that isolation, and human beings refuse to contemplate the possibility that "others" are in some sense "other possible people who dwell or might have dwelt" in or among us. In this process the "other" is externalized and the human response to diversity may be one of conquest or conversion. The long pilgrimage from diversity to pluralism has been replete with these responses, and the human condition is such that pluralism continues to be resisted by programs of conquest and conversion. The culture of religious pluralism has evolved in tension with the impulse to conquer or convert the "other" instead of to contemplate the manner in which the ideas, practices, and sociality of others are aspects of our own incompleteness—indeed, of human incompleteness.

Conquest and the Ritual of Warfare

When the Spanish arrived in the southern part of the continent of North America in the sixteenth century, they encountered two civilizations that were as advanced as societies anywhere else on the planet. The Mayans had an amazing architectural facility, their skill at stone masonry evident in the marvelous temples of Yucatan and Guatemala. Their mathematical abilities were probably more advanced than those of the Greeks, and their calendars were remarkably accurate. Mayan civilization, however, had begun to decline and was challenged by the rising power of the Aztecs. Heirs to the work of other advanced societies like the Mixtec, Toltec, Zapotec, and Teohuacan, the Aztecs ruled over much of what became Mexico and Guatemala. Mayans and Aztecs were peoples who met as "others," and in the course of their encounters, conquest became a model for dealing with human diversity and for resisting the development of pluralism.

When the "other" is totally externalized, it becomes a threat to power, to identity, and to loyalty. If the power that we possess is not recognized as an element that is shared beyond our own possession, then it must be defended against violation. When power is externalized, then we may also covet the power possessed externally by the other. Again, if identity is confined to individuals and groups in total isolation, the presence of the other confounds it. We can only be loyal to the limited selfhood we perceive. Ultimate order and meaning are presumed to depend upon possession of our power, our identity—our gods and our spirits.

Miguel Leon-Portilla, in his restoration of the Aztec account of the Spanish conquest of Mexico, introduces us to the ways in which separate native communities responded to each other and to the marauding Spaniards. The Tlaxcaltecas were enemies of the Cholultecas because the respective powers of their gods and their ways were mutually envied. To consider someone an "enemy" is to convert the "other" into an external entity, thereby justifying hostile action. Leon-Portilla quotes Diego Muñoz Camargo, a Spaniard who married into the nobility of Tlaxcala and wrote from that point of view in his account of the struggle with Cholula,

> which was governed and ruled by two lords, Talquiach and Tlalchiac (for the lords who succeeded to that command were always known by those names, which mean "Lord of what is above" and "Lord of what is below").
>
> Once they entered the province of Cholula, the Spaniards quickly destroyed that city because of the great provocations given by its inhabitants. So many Cholultecas were killed in this invasion that the news raced through the land as far as the City of Mexico. There it caused the most horrible fright and consternation, for it was also known that the Tlaxcaltecas had allied themselves with the "gods" (as the Spaniards were called in all parts of this New World, for want of another name).
>
> The Cholultecas had placed such confidence in their idol Quetzalcoatl that they believed no *human* power could defeat or harm them. They thought they would be able to vanquish us in a very short time. . . . Their faith in the idol was

so complete that they believed it would ravage their enemies with the fire and thunder of heaven, and drown them in a vast flood of water.

This is what they believed, and they proclaimed it in loud voices: "Let the strangers come! We will see if they are so powerful! Our god Quetzalcoatl is here with us, and they can never defeat him. Let them come, the weaklings: we are waiting to see them, and we laugh at their stupid delusions. They are fools or madmen if they trust in these sodomites from Tlaxcala, who are nothing but their women. And let the hirelings come, too: they have sold themselves in their terror. Look at the scum of Tlaxcala, the cowards of Tlaxcala, the guilty ones! They were conquered by the City of Mexico, and now they bring strangers to defend them! How could you change so soon? How could you put yourself into the hands of these foreign savages? Oh, you frightened beggars, you have lost the immortal glory that was won by your heroes, who sprang from the pure blood of the ancient Teochichimecas, the founders of your nation. What will become of you, you traitors? We are waiting, and you will see how our god Quetzalcoatl punishes his foes!"[2]

In this lengthy quotation, we can observe the elements in the structure of conquest, as the "other" is externalized religiously. According to Munoz Camargo, the Cholultecas were "others" who placed "confidence in their idol"; the Spaniards, on the other hand, were both "gods" and "strangers" who did not recognize the power of Quetzalcoatl. The Cholultecas isolated themselves in this way from their neighboring peoples, the Tlaxcaltecas, who were scum, cowards, traitors, sodomites, and women. The way is thus prepared for warfare and possible conquest.

Warfare and conquest, like all human behavior, must be ritualized. Parades of warriors become rituals of boundary making. In ceremonies of dances, vivid colors, and the symbolic brandishing of weapons, one group sets apart the "others" as those whose rituals and worldviews must be deconstructed, perhaps destroyed. Spaniards became aware of Cholultecas as others who possessed what was necessary to their own sanctity of power, and knew that in order for their own lives to be maintained, the Cholultecas (and others all in good time) had to be defeated. Warfare becomes a religious ritual because it is a playing out of the conflict of otherness at work within us and among us. That is to say, the skills, the wealth, and the knowledge that are part of the "other" are thought of as things lost, things of which we have been deprived; but they will be renewed, returned, in the ritual of warfare. Warfare is a ritual of making the other into an enemy because it has what we do not have. It is an alien "other," an externalized, absolute "other," because we do not accept it as part of the multiplicity that is within us. Because we are impatient to get what this "other" has, we ritualize the taking of what the "other as savior" would offer us, or promise to give us in some imaginable future.

The ritual of warfare must not completely *destroy* the other because the other is always part of the multiplicity within us and among us. And the good the other possesses cannot become ours if we destroy the other absolutely. We may wish to conquer, to triumph, to subjugate. But we must be careful. If we utterly annihilate our enemy, we eliminate our own salvation—the means of complementing the multiplicity of our own otherness. Hitler did not understand this at all. His radical attempt to annihilate the Jew as other led to his own destruction. The Jew as the one who remains "outsider," chosen, and unique in his skills of survival is also the Jew of our own otherness. The only possible outcome of a ritual of annihilation will be an extinction, a destruction of the possibility of renewal that lives in our consciousness through this "myth of eternal return."

The Christian story of the death and resurrection of Christ is a radical resolution of the ritual of annihilation conducted by persons like Hitler. In that story the other who is within and among us is forced out. Therefore, the other (God) who is the source of our own being is destroyed, annihilated, crucified. The result is ultimate darkness, a return to the black hole. Only an absolute creative act whereby the other asserts power over annihilation can make creation again possible. Therefore, the resurrection of Christ, in the Christian worldview, affirms the power of otherness over any attempt to destroy it.

When we look at human history (as if there were really any other kind; what, after all, is "natural" history but an imposition of human categories upon the world around us? History involves the accidents and decisions of human existence and their interaction with the ongoing processes of life) we may observe many instances in which conquest and warfare became rituals designed to deal with diversity—the externalized encounter with an other or others who are really part of the multiplicity of our own selfhood.

In a society like ours, humans are deprived of their public power and are left with emotions and dreams that are relegated to the private realms of the nuclear family and the inner self. They struggle to find meaningful community, whether in an imagined past or a contrived present. They find it difficult to discover rituals that are appropriate for the celebration of complete existence; or they experience a certain alienation from those rituals that were supposed to be sufficient for their needs. Living as they do in a raw present where existence is regulated by taxes, jobs, mortgages, auto loans, and credit cards, they are aware of a kind of ongoing, one-damned-thing-after-anotherness to life. They are robbed of a sense of past and of a future lived in harmony with others. This is what Toni Morrison, in her extraordinary novel *Beloved*, calls "rememory":

> You know. Some things you forget. Other things
> you never do. But it's not. Places, places are still

there. If a house burns down, it's gone, but
the place—the picture of it—stays, and not just
in my rememory, but out there, in the world.
What I remember is a picture floating around
out there outside my head. I mean, even if I don't
think it, even if I die, the picture of what I did, or
knew, or saw is still out there. Right in the place
where it happened.[3]

Other people can see it too, says Morrison. There are times when you
hear or see something going on and assume that you're just thinking it
up, like a sort of imagined thing. But what is happening is that you're
bumping into "a memory that belongs to somebody else."

Traditionally, people were attentive to "rememory." They once lived in
communities that were alive to all these things that belonged to them, that
made past, present, and future an affair of lived, substantial reality. Life
was a continuous "bumping into" all kinds of "others" that were never
threatened with annihilation. Even death did not remove them from our
presence. Morrison reminds us in her novel that we must learn to tell the
whole story of rememory, the bumping that is agony as well as bliss, ugly
as well as beautiful, violent as well as peaceful. Contemporary society
does not make it easy to accommodate this sort of sensitivity. We are
robbed of the sense of the interplay of otherness that always extends beyond the present, beyond our own narrow sense of rememory. There are
always rememories "that belong to somebody else," but we bump into
them. They help to shape our own selfhood, the selfhood of *our* people.

Between Conquest and Conversion:
The Case of Christopher Columbus

Christopher Columbus was, presumably, like all or any of us: no better,
no worse. He lived in a world where the things that belonged and the
people he knew were familiar. He "discovered" America by bumping into
a whole set of rememories that belonged to somebody else. He "discovered" it because, like most Europeans, he was hoping to find a world that
fulfilled the expectations, and redeemed the failures, of his own world.
Edmundo O'Gorman has argued against any notion of Columbus "discovering" America.[4] He suggests that it is impossible to discover what
does not exist. Inasmuch as, in the minds of Europeans, there was no map
that envisioned the existence of an American space, no geographical
knowledge of a hidden place waiting to be discovered, there could be no
empirical discovery of America. Amerigo Vespucci was the one who really discovered America, according to O'Gorman. Vespucci's voyage of

1501–1502, along the coast of what is now called South America, convinced him that he had come upon a land previously unknown. In other
words, Columbus found nothing new because he had to reconcile his experiences with the world as it was known to Europeans. Therefore, he
had to adjust his understanding to conform to the charted world. He had
somehow reached the Orient and the inhabitants were "los Indios." The
world of "los Indios" was on the European maps.

Vespucci, on the other hand, recognized that he had discovered something new, something that was not on the maps. The New World he had
discovered began to take its shape, its being, from Vespucci's conception
of it. Because of this fact, it could only be "Amerigo land"—America.

Now, there are several problems with this argument. First of all, what
shall we do with the ambivalence of Columbus's thinking about the matter? "God made me a messenger of the new heaven and new earth of
which He spoke in the Apocalypse by Saint John," he stated in his report
to Prince John, ". . . and He showed me the spot where to find it."[5] The
theology of history inherited by Columbus posited the notion that the
Christian Gospel had to be propagated throughout the whole world before the ultimate goal of history could be reached. In his *Book of Prophecies*,
Columbus affirmed that the end of the world, the consummation of history, could only take place after the *conquest* of the *new* continent, the conversion of its inhabitants, and the destruction of the Antichrist. Strangely,
however, he believed that he had reached the world from which human
history had fallen.

In the mythic understanding of Christianity, human history as we
know it takes place outside the Garden, east of Eden. Yet Eden was still *a
place*, in the minds of most Europeans, beyond the world as they knew it.
It was a *New* World, another world. Columbus was convinced that he had
discovered the New World, just as surely as he thought before that he
could only have found a land that already existed on European maps.
Therein is the ambivalence. And therein lay Columbus's dilemma. How
could he reconcile his cartography, his "Passage to India" (Walt
Whitman's later phrase), with the New World he had discovered? "He
believed," writes Mircea Eliade, "that the fresh water currents he encountered in the Gulf of Paria originated in the four rivers of the Garden of
Eden."[6]

The swarthy people who curiously eyed Columbus from the shores, or
darted in and out among the trees, could only have been the descendants
of the people of the First World. They could only have been the children
of Adam and Eve, their naked innocence a sign of their original virtue.
Imagine for a moment! If that vision of Columbus's discovery had persisted, it could have meant that he and his European companions had
bumped into a rememory of who and what human beings were really

meant to be. It would have been like what Loren Eiseley was talking about when he reminded us that "modern man" does not contemplate "his otherness, the multiplicity of other possible men *who dwell or might have dwelt in Him.*" It would have meant that Columbus had contemplated the other, the "native," as one who dwells within and among us. Meeting the "other" and becoming aware of the diversity of peoples and places would have stretched his worldview to include rememories of Eden, of the New World that was the Paradise Lost.

Historians like O'Gorman must remember that myth and legend are as much the "stuff" of history as the seemingly empirical data of persistent sleuthing and measurement. What a civilization imagines the world to be like determines the language and character of their science and their philosophy. Myth is the imaginative sense of the ultimate order and meaning of existence; and legends are the legitimate offspring of myth, conceived and nurtured in everyday occurrences. There is no history that does not include myth and legend. They belong to the empirical data of existence. They are the interconnections of imagination, reason, and sensory awareness. They make Toni Morrison's rememories something that we can actually "bump into."

"Discovery" is, therefore, not some blatant, raw, sensory encounter; not for human beings, at any rate. "Discovery" also incorporates the expectations and memories of those who meet, those who discover each other. It would have been impossible for Columbus to have discovered *anything except* what he was enabled to perceive on the basis of the imagined order and meaning of the world of which he was a part. Whether he "discovered" the New World or the Orient is impossible to determine, a fact that is demonstrated by the confluence of Edenic notions and existing cartographic knowledge in his attempt to understand his experience. One can never discover raw empirical reality; one discovers *perceptions* of reality.

What is important to our purposes is that Europeans now had to make room in their worldview for "other" peoples who existed in a land that was very much an element in their worldview. If the "native others" were, indeed, the descendants of Adam and Eve in some historically empirical fashion, then they had to be accepted with respect and honor. They had to become the models for Europeans to emulate if they hoped to return to their own innocence in Paradise. The redemption they had been seeking was on the verge of fulfillment.

On the other hand, what were Europeans to make of their own achievements, their civilization? Had the Holy Catholic Church and Empire not created a culture of high philosophy, art, law, and science? Certainly the Lord of history could not simply discard that culture of salvation in favor of a return to naked simplicity. Perhaps the New World waited for the Europeans to *use* it. Perhaps its inhabitants were the poor and ignorant

remnants of an unadvanced society, those in need of salvation—"sal-
vages" (savages). It was even possible to envision these people as decep-
tive, duplicitous members of Satan's militia, children of darkness com-
missioned to thwart the message of Santa Fe (the Holy Faith).

When the latter ideas begin to take precedence in one's imagination,
the "other" becomes the adversary, the one to be converted or conquered.
What could very well remain a "multiplicity of others" *within* and among
us (as Eiseley puts it) becomes instead a plurality of externals. Tzvetan
Todorov, in *The Conquest of America*, informs us that Columbus's primary
concern in his voyages was to acquire the gold that would finance his
dream to lead a crusade to liberate Jerusalem, the Holy City, from the
domination of infidel "others," the Muslims.[7] The success of his crusade
would fulfill a religious longing—it would ensure his eternal salvation
and calm the turbulence of his anguished soul. The native "others" of the
New World became the key to his *spiritual search for gold:* they stood in his
way. At first, they were "very gentle and ignorant of evil," according to
Columbus. They "do not even know how to kill one another. . . . They are
very ready to say the prayers that we teach them and to make the sign of
the Cross."[8] Therefore, they awaited conversion, according to Todorov's
interpretation of the Columbian motivations. They could be persuaded to
become Christians, and share their gold with Columbus and the Holy
Church on behalf of a pious crusade. But the natives did not entirely understand much less *accept* their designated "otherness." They began to resist, because something was being imposed upon them. Ultimately we
can only accept that otherness that we see *in ourselves;* we find it impossible to accept an "otherness" arbitrarily imposed from without.

Signification, Conquest, and Conversion

According to Charles Long, when we "signify" we provide an identity for
an "other"—an identity that the "other" has no hand in fashioning. We assume a position of power for ourselves and our community that controls
our subsequent relationship with the "other." Once we have decided that
an other is "Indian" or "primitive" or "ignorant," the relationship becomes arbitrary. There is little honest discourse from that point on. "The
signifier," writes Long, "may speak in an agreement with a point of view,
while the tone of voice creates doubt in the very act and words of agreement."[9] Of course, this is partly a matter of language; and human relations
would be impossible without a certain amount of signification. After all,
signification has to do with the ordering of society. In order for a university to exist, there must be those who are signified as "students" and others as "professors." But in an ideal social situation, the student and the
professor may close ranks. Students should be encouraged to have a voice

in their own signification. They may become teachers and professors may become students. In much of our discourse and relations, however, the process of signification remains an exercise of power. It resembles the double identity W.E.B. DuBois referred to in his *The Souls of Black Folk*. Custom and legal structures reinforced the role that one community imposed upon another in an act of arbitrary signification. "It is a peculiar sensation," wrote DuBois, "this double-consciousness, this sense of always looking at one's self through the eyes of others, of measuring one's soul by the tape of a world that looks on in amused contempt and pity. One feels his twoness—an American, a Negro; two souls, two thoughts, two unreconciled strivings; two warring ideals in one dark body."[10] One is signifier; the other signified. One is superior; the other inferior.

The act of signification soon justifies conquest or conversion. Columbus was at first ready to acknowledge the natives as "gentle and ignorant of evil,"[11] which, of course, they probably were not. Columbus was signifying so that he might understand them in a way that would help him claim the gold that would ensure his own salvation. At first his signification was modest, but it forced a double identity, a "double-consciousness," upon the native Americans he had encountered. And this modest signification helped to develop a rhetoric by means of which the people of the Americas came to be identified. Instead of accepting the plurality of human being and circumstance, Columbus as the signifier created "other" beings in the image of his own desires and expectations. People who were "like" Columbus in upbringing and motivation shared in the rhetoric of signification. This permitted Europeans to be "parents" of the childlike, converters of heathens, colonizers of the "undeveloped" lands, and conquerors of the enemy.

Todorov tells us that the Spaniards faced a similar sense of signification when they arrived in Mexico City in the early sixteenth century.[12] Cortés had learned of the Aztec empire and its sovereign Montezuma. He took the sovereign prisoner without great resistance. Montezuma chose to abandon his leadership, privileges, and wealth in order to avoid seeing his empire fall into disorder. For some curious reason not known to historians, Montezuma had decided that Cortés and his minions were "friends" or ministers of some strange justice. However, it is important to consider the diversity of the peoples of Mexico at that time. There were numerous native American societies, all of which had been already conquered and colonized by the Aztecs. Montezuma had imposed a precarious unity upon this diverse population. He sought to avoid the disorder that would result from a Spanish conquest, because order is essential to meaningful existence and because it would be better to have the Spaniards as allies than to invite a chaotic invasion and the retribution of the "other" native American peoples.

The Soul of Conversion

Plurality usually requires some kind of human response because order and power are involved. Order is a fundamental human and religious necessity. As Mircea Eliade has shown us, human beings have had to fix the limits and boundaries of their world, to organize their world according to some model of the ultimate.[13] They have established order over, *against*, and in relation to what is "outside," other, and even what is chaos. Every human habitation reflects the imagined order of a people, a society. The habitation reminds us: This is who we are; this is our place, our world; this is inviolate; the "outside" is not a world like ours; you can exist in my real world only if I invite you in, only if I *convert* you to "one of us."

Conversion is an unusual business. Many of the intellectuals of the modern world (1500–1920), in their reaction against the old order of Christianity, have bequeathed us their biases. In this postmodern era, the intellectuals ask the Christian, "What right have you to try to convert us, to tell us your way is the better, or the only way?" But conversion goes on all the time, does it not? When I become aware of others who are outside my world, I seek to invite them in. That is certainly one form of conversion. When you become my friend and visit me in my world (the one I have decorated and occupied and for which I have created rules of hospitality), you *turn* your life *together with* mine. You are no longer an outsider. Our worlds have been turned about, converted, put together in a new way. It is true that many Christian groups have advocated a different model of conversion. They have insisted that you *give up* whatever character, identity, and comportment you represent and adopt their world absolutely. There have been times, periods, and places in which Orthodox, Roman Catholic, and Protestant Christians have had this kind of expectation as they faced diversity and failed to contemplate their own otherness. Conversion then becomes a matter of turning from who one is and becoming the other who confronts us. Evangelical Christians tend to insist upon this model of conversion, at least in their rhetoric. But it is only *one* model; and history has demonstrated its inadequacy.

Evangelical Christians living in Texas or the mountains of Tennessee do *not* speak, act, or think like those Christians who are members of the Riverside Church or the St. Thomas Episcopal Church in New York City. Both groups may include "converts," but their models of conversion are different. The fact that the models differ indicates that no one really converts absolutely—in the sense that we give up entirely who and what we are and value. Two models of conversion—the one a turning together, the other an absolute turning away from one and to another—are demonstrated in the course of history. In a way, there is a third. Most Americans are aware of the term "conversion" as it applies to the national sport of football. Its implicit meaning is helpful to our purpose.

When a team has made its way across its opponent's goal line, it has achieved its purpose: It has scored a touchdown, worth six points. But this accomplishment can be extended, or supplemented. The scoring team has the opportunity to "convert" six points into seven or eight. The additional one or two points are impossible without first getting the six with a touchdown, but the touchdown has the potential to be converted into "more."

When we examine the history of religion in America, we discover numerous instances in which the encounters between diverse ways of life have resulted in a mode of conversion such as that described above. Native Americans have been difficult to "convert" in the sense of an absolute turning *from* their traditional ways *to* (for example) an evangelical Christian faith that rejects native tradition as magical, superstitious, demonic, or "pagan." The Franciscan friars of the Roman Catholic Church had great difficulty converting the Pueblo peoples of New Mexico. The friars maintained a notion of exclusive loyalty and had little use for the traditional ways of the Pueblos.

Parenthetically, it should be pointed out that part of the reason for Christian exclusivism, of course, has derived from the history of European warfare. Christianity developed in a world of considerable mobility and struggle among nations, much of the movement and aggression channeled toward imperialistic domination. When early Christians existed in relatively small enclaves under the surveillance of Roman authorities, they thought of themselves as communities of those who were "*in*, but not *of* the world." Their sense of solidarity and close community was forced upon them by their precarious existence in a hostile world. By way of martyrdom they demonstrated the uniqueness of their claims— they were *Christ's* martyrs, suffering His death with Him in a world that rejected Him. Martyrdom became a sign of "chosenness." Early Christianity developed its exclusiveness in a manner similar to that of the Jews. Before the time of the Emperors Constantine and Theodosius (fourth century C.E.), Jews and Christians experienced similar (though certainly not identical) formations of their identities in the pluralistic world of the Roman Empire. Both had to articulate the significance of their rejection by that Empire. Certainly much of the understanding of Jewish chosenness was fashioned in the context of rejection, first by Rome, then by sixteen centuries of the hegemony of Christendom.

We remember that the presence of plural claims to the order and meaning of existence raises the question of identity. Trying to clarify who we are and how our world is ordered are serious preoccupations in a society of diversity. The many varieties of Christianity are evidence of these preoccupations. Christian history *in the European and American settings* manifests the result of first having been rejected, then emerging triumphant in the social, political, and cultural world. As we consider the radical diversity of the twenty-first century that faces us, we will begin to see modifications of Christian exclusivism as well as a resurgence of conservative exclusivism among those whose identity is profoundly threatened by a world where Christianity is often relegated to the realm of private experience.

The Franciscan friars, who attempted to convert the Pueblos, were advocates of the exclusive character of Christianity. Henry Bowden informs us that the Pueblo Indians of New Mexico were "conditioned to conformity since childhood, [and] accepted the new social forces that had entered their culture like the point of a wedge."[14] However, their "conformity" was not absolute; they were more syncretistic than conformist. That is to say, they were a people with long experience of adjustment and accommodation to the stories, rituals, and technologies of other peoples. However, the Pueblos were not accustomed to *giving up* their own *tradition*, their own knowledge of the ultimate order and meaning of existence. Like many other Native American nations (the Yaqui, for example), they were a people who "kicked extra points." Conversion was a matter of adding to, or completing, what they had already been given by their ancestors. Conversion was complementary and supplementary. As Bowden admits: "The Pueblos did not know that the Spaniards planned to use their initial accommodations as the means of transforming native life into their own model of civilization, including its religion."[15]

As a people become aware of a multiplicity of claims about the ultimate order and meaning of existence, they are faced with the necessity of responding to those others whose claims seem to render them a separate people. If they find it difficult to discern those others as elements in their own selfhood, they will reject the ideas and ways of those others. Two models of response to religious diversity that emerge in such circumstances are those of conquest and conversion. We have examined the inner sense of these models and hopefully have shown how they are never totally absent from human behavior. Pluralism is difficult to accept. It is not easy to contemplate "the multiplicity of other people who dwell or might have dwelt" in and among us. Pluralism requires a religious sensibility that recognizes the symbolic character of religion and culture, the manner in which these human achievements point beyond themselves to a reality that makes the acceptance of others a creative probability. Conquest and conversion are sometimes responses to diversity that allow us to try to possess what cannot ultimately be possessed—the otherness of our own selfhood.

Notes

1. Loren Eiseley, *The Night Country* (New York: Charles Scribner's Sons, 1971), p. 148.

2. Miguel Leon-Portilla, *The Broken Spears* (Boston: Beacon Press, 1992), pp. 43–44.

3. Toni Morrison, *Beloved* (New York: Penguin, 1987), p. 36.

4. Edmundo O'Gorman, *The Invention of America* (Bloomington: Indiana University Press, 1961), p. 2.

5. Mircea Eliade, *The Quest* (Chicago: University of Chicago Press, 1969), p. 91.

6. Eliade, p. 90.

7. Tzvetan Todorov, *The Conquest of America* (New York: Harper & Row, 1984), pp. 11–13.

8. Todorov, p. 44.

9. Charles H. Long, *Significations* (Philadelphia: Fortress Press, 1986), p. 1.

10. W.E.B. DuBois, *The Souls of Black Folk* (New York: Signet Books, 1969), p. 45.

11. Todorov, p. 44.

12. Todorov, chap. 2.

13. See Mircea Eliade, *The Sacred and the Profane* (New York: Harcourt Brace & Company, 1959), chap. 1.

14. Henry W. Bowden, *American Indians and Christian Missions* (Chicago: University of Chicago Press, 1981), p. 42.

15. Bowden, p. 43.

3

The Denominational Model: From Dissent to Commonality

It is when we give our attention to the question of the unity and diversity within the limited area that we know best, and within which we have the most frequent opportunities for right action, that we can combat the hopelessness that invades us, when we linger too long upon perplexities so far beyond our measure.[1]

—T. S. Eliot, "Notes Toward the Definition of Culture"

Although human societies still tend to respond to religious and cultural diversity aggressively, through conquest and conversion, we are always conscious of the need to move beyond our natural inclinations in this regard. T. S. Eliot suggests that the issues of unity and diversity cannot be contemplated in an idealistic or abstract manner, but only "within the limited area that we know best, and within which we have the most frequent opportunities for right action." In other words, we must arrive at some workable context in the struggle to deal with unity and diversity. By affirming only some vague ideal of transcendence or unity, we become revolutionaries in defense of an unrealizable society or rationalists with little or no effect on life itself. The contemplation of our otherness must take place in a particular context. As Eliot puts it, we can only recognize the significance of both unity and diversity from within a *particular* area; we can only *do something* about these matters—genuinely contemplate our otherness—if we stand within human circumstances that make the problem real. I can only have an appreciative consciousness of the multiplicity of others, I can only wonder at the richness of my own tradition, if I stand within to examine others and contemplate the significance of this posture. Accordingly, there is no escaping the dilemma that pluralism seeks to resolve. To ignore the significance of those who stand within the limited area of a religious and cultural tradition is to judge them as benighted or ignorant; such an approach contributes little that is substantial to the resolution of matters of unity and diversity.

In the early stages of European-American history there developed a serious response to diversity that sought to approach the matter by standing "within the limited area" that was best known. The idea of the "denomination" emerged as the basis for appropriate actions that could be taken from this limited perspective. The denomination slouches toward pluralism, and might be considered a contextually historical realization of it; however, its time is up because the circumstances of its birth have been transcended.

The representatives of denominations always know that they are one among many. In the American context the denomination has had a distinctively "institutional" character; it has been a conscious incorporation, an "appropriate action" in relation to certain religious claims and practices. "The denomination," writes Sidney Mead, "unlike the traditional forms of the Church, is not primarily confessional, and it is certainly not territorial. Rather it is purposive, and unlike any previous Church in Christendom, it has no official connection with a civil power whatsoever."[2] Mead here provides us with the language necessary to analyze the significance of the term. "Denomination" is a term of Christian origin. It is not confessional, meaning that it does not arise in order to represent a distinctive set of propositional teachings as, for example, did Lutheranism with its reliance upon the Augsburg Confession as a definitive statement of faith. And it is not territorial, says Mead, meaning that it is not a sacred order of a particular place or nation, that it is not politically ordered. Of course, the argument could be made that the denomination *is* territorial in the sense that it has arranged the patterns of religious life in America. Although we are thus provided with a basis for an understanding of the concept of the denomination, we shall see that the word has a history subsequent to its origin and that there may be times and situations in which denomination is not confined to Christianity and may even become somewhat confessional. Denominationalism emerges in the course of the endeavor to find a workable consensus in the midst of dissent and differentiation.

Denominations of Dissenters

The denomination is basically a Christian concept; in fact, it is *Puritan* Christian, its origins linked to the English Reformation. The latter event generated the Puritan movement with its great diversity of opinion and practice in seventeenth-century England as well as in colonial America. In England, Parliament sought to bring this plurality of Christian claims into some kind of workable settlement. Those reformers who dissented from the majority opinion of the Church began to resolve their differences. "Though our differences are sad enough," they said, "yet they come not up to this to make us men of different religions. We agree in the same end though not in the same means. They are but different ways of opposing the common enemy, would be very comfortable. It would be our strength. But that cannot be expected in this world."[3]

These dissenting reformers were shaping the concept of the denomination. If a nomination is a naming, an adherence to a certain name, a certain way, a certain "end," then a *de*nomination becomes *a part of* that naming, or what the dissenters called a different "means" of serving the same end, "opposing the *common* enemy." In this way the word "denomination" came into use in both England and America, so that by the eighteenth century John Wesley, the "founder" of Methodism, could detest all distinctions among Christians: "I . . . refuse to be distinguished from other men by any but the common principles of Christianity. . . . I renounce and detest all other marks of distinction. But from real Christians, of whatever *denomination*, I earnestly desire not to be distinguished at all."[4]

The sentiment behind Wesley's statement was that the different "means" that characterized a denomination were of no real consequence in considering one's loyalty to the "common principles of Christianity." This is a debatable point, of course; but it was not so to Wesley, and it became a common attitude among American Christians dedicated to the evangelical mission of converting individuals as Christ's disciples. "All societies who profess Christianity," said the American revivalist Gilbert Tennent, "and retain the foundational principles thereof, notwithstanding their different denominations and diversity of sentiments in smaller things, are in reality but one Church of Christ [one nomination] but several branches (more or less pure in minuter points) of one visible kingdom of the Messiah."[5]

Denominations of Common Principles

By the middle of the eighteenth century (Tennent's time), a certain essentialism had taken root in American thinking. The notion that there were "foundational principles" (or Wesley's "common principles") had become a prominent assumption for the style of Protestant Christianity that was becoming prominent in the emerging nation. Foundational or common principles were thought to be the "essence" of Christianity, the essential truth beneath all phenomenological differences. By the end of the eighteenth century this religious essentialism had been reduced to what Benjamin Franklin and Thomas Jefferson were prone to call the *essentials* of every religion, the principle beliefs and assumptions found in every religion in the country. We can understand this assertion of essentialism as a move in the direction of pluralism. However, the form of essentialist thinking common to Franklin, Jefferson, and the American Enlightenment was a derivative of Christian history and not yet presented in a sufficiently radical context. It was an essentialism seeking to make sense of a Biblical and Christian diversity.

We must remember that the real revolution then occurring in America was not the war that began in 1776, but the radical change in the old European ways of thinking and acting. This change was occasioned by an emphasis upon individual decision and experience that emerged out of English Puritanism and continental Protestantism. The emphasis was in harmony with the ideas generated by the birth of the modern world and was observed in certain Renaissance notions, Newtonian and Baconian science, and the Enlightenment. The real American revolution was organically grown along the hedgerows of the American landscape.

In North America the long-standing European traditions of education, church order, social class, and designated leadership did not seem to apply. Instead, America provided Europeans of all walks of life with the opportunity to rely upon their own resources. The British Isles and the European mainland, with their centuries-old established ways, were thousands of miles to the east, across ominous waters that complied only reluctantly with human expectations. In the American wilderness of the eastern seaboard there were no bishops, no kings, few colleges, and no ordaining agencies. The people were farmers, craftsmen, and members of the rising middle class of commercial entrepreneurs and tradesmen. They were in a hurry to establish some pattern of existence that would enable them to survive and, hopefully, prosper. Even organized religion had to be adapted to promote successful living, and in most locations adjusted to grassroots leadership. Ideas and beliefs, as well as attitudes toward behavior and ritual practices, were nurtured in this revolutionary setting. In fact, historians like Edwin Gaustad have shown that certain nontraditional convictions and practices, spawned in the religious life of colonial America, were the lifeblood of the struggle for independence from English governance.[6] It seems obvious that the revolutionary setting of eighteenth-century America tended to level many of the traditional and distinctive notions of religion and politics that were the heritage of European Americans.

This leveling was expressed in the development of the idea of the denomination *and* in the tendency to assume that common essentials lay beneath all denominational differences. To admit that we are a denomination of the fullness of the Church of Christ is also to acknowledge that our distinctive teachings and practices are not of primary significance. The way is open to notions of an essential religion behind the facade of particularity. Tennent's and Wesley's ideas of the "real Christians" drawn from many denominations are not far from Franklin's "essentials common to every religion" or to the basic practical Christianity fostered in many denominations by the democratic leadership of a revolutionary nation.

Denomination as Institution

Denominationalism is a uniquely American response to plural claims to religious truth. Of course, the denomination functions in numerous ways and has meant different things at various stages of our history. The denomination is, after all, an institution. Whatever else human beings are, they are institution builders, and perhaps nowhere in the geography of the planet has this characteristic been demonstrated as well as in the United States. Americans have been insistent, activistic, and extensive institution builders. American institutions are models of socialization that are at once both legal entities and purposive self-sustaining organizations. People institute in order to regularize, regulate, and sustain a certain vision or purpose. If and when we agree that a certain insight or ideal is crucial to life's purpose, or that some human need must be addressed, we will feel compelled to institute a means of realizing the ideal or the appropriate program of action. Institutionalization is simply facilitation with a sense of continuity.

The forms of religious institutions that existed before the American War of Independence and the birth of the new republic were transformed by the social, political, and religious realities of the *novus ordo seclorum*, the new society for the world—an affirmation on the Great Seal of the United States, where the words *annuit coeptis* ("our undertaking is favored") were also imprinted. Although the new society had been long in the making, it was new in its mandate for a changed institutional life. Even the denominations were different before the Constitutional Divide. There had been an organic character to the institutions of colonial America. They were bodies, units of broadened identity and almost communal order. However, the society of the new republic demanded efficiency. It required a collectivization of individuals. In a sense, individuals were to come together to fashion associations, instead of the more organic notion of individuals existing as elements of community created *by* community. In order for the new nation to build up its society, to get the jobs done that were required for survival and success, a new type of institution was needed. Efficiency, competition, and success were the new criteria. Associations of people needed to be hastily and voluntarily put together, their members committed by way of shared experience and dedication to common goals. The associations existed only as collectivities of individuals, not as a priori organic units like the family, the people of Israel, or the church of European Christendom. They had to be highly efficient, popular, and democratic in order to survive. They were to exist by legal mandate only so long as they continued to be efficient.

Whether these new definitive institutions were congregations of evangelical Christians or voluntary societies for the instituting of education, temperance, peace, or antislavery reform, they had a religious foundation and were to have a distinctive organizational identity.[7] The denominations were no longer units of a common nomination of Christ. The term was applied to the notion of independent organizations bent on survival and charged with the self-perpetuating claims of a set of distinctive teachings and practices. The diversity of nineteenth-century religious life was replete with feverish activity.

Many of us are familiar with the story of Joseph Smith, the youthful, charismatic founder of the Church of Jesus Christ of Latter-day Saints, or the Mormons. Smith lived in what historians have called the "burned over district" of western New York State.[8] Early nineteenth-century revivals raged like brush fires over that part of the country, leaving a trail of enthusiastic and twice-born souls, all waiting for the next spiritual "high." In the wake of the revivals, the denominations grew and entered into competition for the twice-born. Young Joseph Smith underwent a transforming experience in the revival fires of the burned over district. But he was restless and troubled. "O Lord, which of the churches shall I join? The Presbyterians, the Baptists, the Methodists? Which?" There was an answer to Joseph's prayer: "Join none of them. Each is equally false and removed from the truth that shall be revealed to you."[9]

Joseph's revelation enabled him to leap back across centuries of falsehood to a lost faith that was waiting to be restored on the North American continent. It had been waiting for the birth of the new American republic. The Church of Jesus Christ of Latter-day Saints was an attempt to rise above denominations, to put an end to the unwarranted Protestant diversity. The emergence of this religious movement illustrates the frustration that often accompanies the experience of diversity. Instead of accepting denominational status in the earlier Puritan manner, the Mormon church sought to rise above diversity by reconstituting a lost history. By the time the movement had emerged, American religious and cultural life had been significantly institutionalized. As a result, the Mormons added one more organization, or denomination, to the multitude that Joseph Smith had sought to transcend. The rise of the Latter-day Saints helped to alter the meaning of the word denomination; it now could refer to any institution that was part of the diversity of American religion.

In the early nineteenth century the denominations organized their intercongregational structures. They established careful statistical records of "membership," financial, and property resources. Of course, there had been parish records of baptisms, marriages, and burials in Europe, England, and colonial America. But the fastidious regard for membership was related to the need for institutional justification in the new republic. Membership records demonstrated growth or decline, success or failure. Congregations depended for their continued existence on the support of a constituency, not upon their status within an established religious order. But they also depended upon the status and connections of an effective denomination, which could provide a ready-made constituency of worshippers in the transient circumstances of an expanding frontier nation. And, of course, denominations also depended upon the continued success of their congregations. The new institutions developed managerial orders, people who devoted their professional lives to the specialized tasks required to run any efficient organization. Yet throughout the nineteenth century the old denominational ideology persisted. Institutions competing for constituencies still sought to make interdenominational alliances and to speak of the common Christian ground that lay beneath their separate foundations.

Denominations as a United Front

Denominationalism provided common ground in the face of any threat to the religious and social détente of the largely Protestant and "common essentials" culture. When the immigration movements of the 1830s and 1840s enlarged the range of religious and cultural diversity by bringing large numbers of German Jews and Irish Catholics onto American shores, denominationalism provided a united front against the "evils" of Roman Catholicism and assisted in the socialization of Jews into the Reform Judaism of the Pittsburgh Platform of 1885.

The Irish were Roman Catholics. They were representatives of an alien culture, a culture that had remained essentially Catholic after the Reformation of the sixteenth century. Catholic cultures tended to preserve elements of folk religion that were denied as superstitious and unchristian by the Protestant and Anabaptist forces unleashed during the Reformation. Much of Protestantism had considered the Pope to be anti-Christ* and the Roman Church to be a bastion of magic, superstition, ignorance, and insidious activity. Anti-Catholicism had been a part of Protestant and American Enlightenment rhetoric and thought since the sixteenth century. It had been enough for Protestants and Anabaptists in America to accept the presence of the French, whose religious life seemed to be a secularized Catholicism that desecrated the Sunday Sabbath with picnics, frivolity, and even work. The Irish were another matter. They were a tempestuous peasantry who went to Mass but brawled and drank and otherwise seemed unfit for the propriety, decorum, and industriousness of the Protestant republic. Thus was born an attitude of "nativism"

---

*The notion that evil often masquerades as good, pretending to represent Christ the Savior while contributing to the cause of the Evil One, Satan.

that sought to discredit foreigners whose presence threatened the secure world of the settled "native" Protestant and Enlightenment diversity. Some nativist activity was marked by vigilantism and distorted propaganda. But there was also a more moderate form of resistance to the alleged alien threat. The denominations forged a stronger alliance that sought to present a united front, hoping through evangelism, education, and social reform to prevent the erosion of their religious foundations and perhaps to transform the aliens into religiously homogeneous Americans.

Modernization and the End
of the Old Denomination

The process of modernization continued in America almost unabated throughout the nineteenth and twentieth centuries. Industrialization, accompanied by large-scale movements of people from Europe to America and characterized by increased urbanization, was fashioning a nation quite different from Jonathan Edwards's Massachusetts, Jefferson's Virginia, or Ralph Waldo Emerson's Brahmin New England. Since the nineteenth century, America has been a kind of microcosm of what has been happening to the rest of the planet. The religious and cultural diversity that was largely regionalized in distinct ethnic or national sacred landscapes in Asia, Africa, Europe, and the Middle East has been mobilized, accelerated. Diversity has become migratory, its possible tensions magnified by existence in a nation where the landscape, the place, belongs to no one people, where American Indians are the only peoples with any claim to sacred landscape. America's religious diversity contributes to the privatization of religion and dictates the public definition of religion as something that can be done anywhere; sacred space is denied as an element in the communal expression of religion.

The diversity of religious life in America deconstructs religion itself. The importance of sacred space can only be an attribute of a pluralism that understands the American landscape as a sacred refuge for all peoples. Human community is difficult to experience in relation to specific neighborhoods and geographical locations. Exceptions are to be found in long-established enclaves such as the Hasidic Jewish settlement in Williamsburg, Brooklyn. Newer neighborhoods reflect the radical diversity that has more recently characterized America, especially since 1965. A given neighborhood may have Hindus from India, Muslims from the Near East or Southeast Asia, Buddhists from Thailand or Vietnam, and evangelical Christians from Texas. Whatever community emerges from such a mixed society as this will most likely be in conflict with the patterns of sacred and profane behavior nurtured in the separate religious and ethnic societies that existed before immigration and that must now learn to function as denominations and religious institutions in modern America.

Denominations no longer exist as *de*nominations of common essentials derived from Christian origins; they are no longer expressive of a specific religious reality that is assumed to be fundamental to the process of making human life more human. This transformation can only be reversed to the extent that pluralism reaches religious maturity in relation to the sacredness of the American landscape. Meanwhile, the *institutional* form of the denomination has won out. Denominations remain as functional religious corporations. They represent collectivities of congregations that are themselves processors of the private experiences and self-esteem of individuals who must serve the new religious center of civilization—the corporation and its technological monastic strongholds.

Denominations as Centers of Discourse and Identity

There is something else to consider in thinking about denominations as expressions of, or responses to, diversity. However irrelevant they may seem in relation to public centers of power like the state, the corporation, and the research institute, the denominations remain as centers of discourse and identity. Identity is an important element in a fragmented society where people have little say about how they will spend their time and their lives and what they will value. Although the media serve as the educational arm of modern American society, teaching the values necessary to corporate and technological authority, they ignore the denominations ultimately to their own detriment. The denominations serve as enclaves of conspiracy, helping people raise questions: Is this all there is? Am I no more than what this society says I am? Who am I?

The issue of identity, as discussed earlier, is basically a social matter that only arises when the organic components of existence do not work for us. When family, race, ethnicity, church, nation, and ritual process no longer stand in apposition to us, thus providing a comfortable drama of selfhood in which we have a role to play, then we undergo identity crises. In the modern world, our associations tend to be contractual, contrived, and unstable. They are job related and often temporary; they are not organic relationships that are taken for granted. The most effective kind of identity is expressed with a statement like, "I am Dinéh." To say this is to acknowledge that my identity is *of this people*. The 1960s in America was a decade during which people were in search of identity. The old warrants were questioned, the old commitments and loyalties under siege. In the cartoons of Abner Dean, in the music of the Beatles and Simon and Garfunkel, and in the rhetoric of the "new morality" and the theater of

the absurd, a struggle for identity was expressed. "Who is the real ר.
was a persistent question. The image of a captive inner identity was constant. One could imagine individuals with heads bowed, poised to gaze
inward whenever the outer shell of the navel was peeled away and the
gate was opened to pure and untrammeled identity. What the soul seek-
ers did not comprehend was that the most effective acknowledgment of
identity was the one *rejected* by the rhetoric of revolution:

> *I am Dorothy, daughter of Estelle and Henry Snyder.*
> *I am a Lutheran from Womelsdorf, Pennsylvania,*
> *where the family always gathers on Memorial Day*
> *and Thanksgiving.*

In a society where there is little time for organic relationships to sustain
our identity, a measure of identity formation is left to the private domain
of existence. If I am dissatisfied with the manner in which government,
job, and commercial interests have usurped the time I need to nurture my
identity, I might turn to a religious organization. Today these organizations are designed to address the needs of individual consumers who
turn to them for identity and acceptance. Identity is always a religious
matter because it involves our ultimate meaningful placement in an ordered world. Whether a rhetoric of identity is used or not, the message
and the ritual life of denominations are concerned with helping us know
who we are in the ultimate scheme of things.

No form of communication other than television touches the lives of as
many people on a regular basis as America's congregations and denominations. Although most modern Americans participate in institutional religious life while retaining their own private spiritual, moral, and "theological" agendas, they often find a way to affirm those agendas by
attending the services, classes, and programs of the myriad denominations. Much of the worship and educational life of these institutions has
been altered to suit the private search for identity and self-esteem. The
classical doctrine and liturgy of earlier traditional Christianity, for example, have been transformed into ideas and meditational skills designed to
instill a sense of success and achievement. As a matter of fact, denominational religious life in America continues to be very vital.

The New Denominationalism

As in the days of the new republic, however, competition and the need to
succeed still define much of our religious life. New congregations and new
denominations are constantly emerging. The sacred landscape of America
is radically changed. The spires of Congregational and Presbyterian

churches may continue to be part of a landscape that was shaped during the colonial period. And St. Mary's Catholic Church, which graces the inner-city skyline of Phoenix, Arizona, is still a recognized monument to Spanish mission architecture. But a different kind of sacralization of the landscape has been occurring since the turn of the twentieth century. The birth of the Holiness and Pentecostal movements is further evidence of an emerging democratic people's religion that bypasses the classical shape of Reformation Protestantism, Roman Catholicism, and Eastern Orthodoxy.

These congregations and denominations are not Protestant. They are a form of charismatic and moralistic religion that is generated by people's demands for experiences that support and motivate their social and economic conditions. They have not emerged as representations of common essentials; rather, they produce their own leadership and find release from the anxieties and tensions of contemporary existence. They sacralize the skyline with megachurches with huge theater-like buildings designed to enhance the color, entertainment, and excitement of their message of salvation and success. The membership of these congregations often numbers in the thousands, often as high as ten or twenty thousand. Religion is not dead in this seemingly secular age. Instead it often becomes the Religion of Personal and Spiritual "Success" in a culture that determines success by economic and technological means.

But not all of this new religion is found in megachurches. A storefront can also be a sacred center that provides consultation, classes, and some variation of worship for hundreds of people who inhabit the inner city or who are drawn to some promise of spiritual success and self-esteem. A former roller skating arena can become a very posh and glamorous setting for religious video, aerobic faith, films, and celebrity appearances. Workshops for the assurance of salvation and the joy of repentance also take us step-by-step through a process designed to make us happy and healed. We are taught how salvation makes good business sense. Potter's Houses, Art of Living Family Worship Centers, and The Door comprise only a small percentage of the new religious institutions that have altered the sacred landscape of America. Along with hundreds of small congregations that often use conventional architecture or occupy buildings abandoned by Baptists, Methodists, and Presbyterians, they offer a profile of the new denominationalism.

The village of Strawberry, Arizona, is a typical western American settlement. It sprawls and nestles among the ponderosas and alligator junipers of the Mogollon Rim country. It would be difficult to determine the exact population of Strawberry, although I suppose the power company and the private water company could provide a good starting count. The fate of Strawberry is currently linked to the town of Pine that concentrates its inhabitants three miles away at a lower elevation. The area was settled by

Latter-day Saints during the latter part of the nineteenth century. There is a Mormon church in Pine. Strawberry, on the other hand, has very little in terms of a recognizable sacred landscape. On Fossil Creek Road, about a mile from Highway 87, Strawberry Chapel shares its lighted marquee with the early-evening traffic. Strawberry Chapel is one of the nondenominational evangelical congregations that make up the new denominationalism. There is no center to Strawberry, except for some businesses out on Highway 87. Strawberry Market, the Sportsman's Chalet, a couple of small motels, Charlie T's Eatery, an antique shop, a hair salon, a used clothing shop, an auto repair garage, and the Strawberry Lodge (a rustic hotel, bar, and country restaurant)—that's it. Until recently. The landscape has now changed. Just beyond the Windmill Motor Lodge, the land has been leveled, a rail fence erected, and a long, low hall has appeared along Route 87. The sign before the entrance reads: New Life Foundation. As far as the landscape is concerned, Strawberry, Arizona, is new denominationalism.

If the original purpose of denominationalism was to provide a basis for unity in the midst of diversity, the new denominationalism is to a large extent an exercise in entrepreneurial religion. Religion in America has become primarily a matter of voluntary and private judgment in relation to market opportunities that appeal to our needs, both self-defined and commercially motivated. The diversity of American religion is enhanced by marketplace denominationalism.

This means that a new mode of discourse is being fashioned, even as new forms of identity have emerged. The new denominations are communities of discourse. A certain language is fashioned, images are created, and rhetoric is established that shapes the thought and actions of millions of Americans. Although that rhetoric may be in harmony with the language and values of corporate and technological America, it also might be as concerned with the privacy and judgment of the individual as it is with a vindication of the values of success, happiness, and triumphant competition. The continued participation of Americans in diverse forms of institutional religion is evidence of the fact that Americans' self-understanding and fundamental human needs are at cross purposes. As Robert Bellah and his associates pointed out in their popular book *Habits of the Heart*, Americans espouse a rhetoric of private individualism (what Bellah calls "utilitarian individualism," derived perhaps from the philosophy of Thomas Hobbes) while indicating by their lifestyles and the causes they support that community is an important human requirement.[10]

What are we to make of the fact that millions of Americans who advocate an almost atomistic, solitary individualism participate regularly in the creation and maintenance of denominationalism? Might it not be that all rhetoric requires a community of discourse? Why else would America's extremists find it necessary to belong to reactionary, and often militant, groups of survivalists or "America First" advocates? In some sense this may mean that the language of individualism is at heart a testimony of belonging, a witness to identity. As a human being, I may wish to think that I am not like those others who give in to taxes, to welfare, to a government that sticks its nose into my business. I am not *one of* "those"; I am *one* of these.

Our society is not given to great critical thinking. The kind of powerful economic existence manifested in America and much of the West, and increasingly in much of the world, is not a tribute to analytical or speculative reason. Instead, it has been fashioned by information and technical reason—the ability to work with functional links of ideas. We have often heard that the success of the Japanese in the technology market is due to their ability to follow directions and manipulate minute linkages of data and function. Yet this observation fits much of the emerging global technocorporate society. We have neither the time nor the inclination for speculation, imagination, or careful, probing analysis. My students are completely confused when I tell them that my lectures are not concerned with information, so they had best lay down their pens and listen. When I tell them that information is neither knowledge nor understanding, that I would like them not to use the word "information," I render them theoretically dysfunctional. They are poised to "take down information." When they miss class and call me on the telephone, they ask: "What information did I miss?" "Information" and "data" are modern rhetoric. They are sloganized terms like "access" and "impact," both of which are nouns forced into double duty as verbs in order to satisfy a manipulative mode of discourse that strives to keep our thinking on a functional, technical level.

Advertising has accustomed us to think in terms of slogans. Politics is frequently reduced to bumper stickers. "Eliminate big government!" proclaims one slogan that will likely help elect those who have adopted it. It is highly unlikely that those citizens of the republic who abide by the slogan have done any systematic analysis of the implications of their political stance. The mode of discourse shared by most Americans is sloganized thinking, and this is also true of the new denominationalism.

When I decide to join the First Assembly of God or the Potter's House, or enroll for workshops at the New Life Foundation, it is probably because I have heard someone refer to my new congregation as the church that has something for everyone, as the place where nobody talks down to you, the place that makes a difference, the temple where God helps you tap your untapped power. These institutions do not require us to engage in profound thought or study. They affirm the basic anti-intellectual character of Americans.

The clergy of the so-called mainline denominations have long been working with a form of discourse that is removed from the thinking and expectations of their congregations. It is frequently the case that people leave such services with comments like, "Well, that sermon was way over my head!" or "I certainly didn't agree with that!" The crisis of the old denominations is a crisis of rhetoric—there has been no effective community of discourse. Clergy and congregation do not often share the same language and goals. The result has been that the people retreat into the realms of their private agendas. Even when they happen to like the priest or the minister or the rabbi, they may not hear what he says, but what they think he *should* say. When religious institutions do not nurture a community of discourse, they degenerate; and, in a culture of competitive religious survival, they will probably lose membership, become ineffective, and eventually fold. Of course, the mainline denominations show some evidence of trying to adjust to the sloganized and imagistic orientation of the new denominations. Religious institutions in America have always been amazingly resilient and resourceful, having to survive in an entrepreneurial culture.

As the old denominations begin to adopt the modes of discourse and identity that characterize the new denominations, there emerges a common rhetoric that sounds like New Age and Native American spirituality, an intermixture of popular psychology, occultism, positive thinking, and traditional religious language. One wonders whether the new denominationalism will not only increase religious plurality but also develop a new variety of Franklin's old "common essentials," a new faith that harmonizes with the spirit of technocorporate America. These "new" essentials will still very likely fall short of the religious pluralism required to satisfy the radical diversity characteristic of America's religion and culture.

The Denomination as Denial of the New Denominationalism

In those periods when denominations emerge as institutional varieties of a de-nominated essential religion, there is always dissent and reaction. Denominations not only express a diversity of opportunity and an attempt to harmonize competing claims to the same truth; they also emerge in *opposition* to harmonization. The ecumenical movement that took shape in the twentieth century was a form of the old denominationalism. In the face of a common "secular" enemy and the injustices of urban and industrial society, Christian churches sought to find a means of cooperation. Organizations like the Federal and National Councils of Churches worked with the assumption that there was a common Christian loyalty to Christ as Lord and Savior and as champion of the poor and the oppressed. They first sought to cooperate on a level of action, working together to address social ills and injustice in the name of Christ. Only later did the denominations try to discuss doctrine, teaching, and basic theological differences. The World Council of Churches established a Faith and Order Commission to address doctrinal interpretations of what was assumed to be the common faith expressive of loyalty to Jesus Christ. This was an exercise not unlike earlier attempts by churches to recognize each other as de-nominations of a common nomination of Christ's Church. The participants assumed that the use of Christ's name implied an underlying commonality of thought and practice. They did not entertain the notion that there may be many Christianities with nothing more in common than a name. They did not consider the possibility that some Christians may have more in common with Jews or Buddhists than with fellow "Christians." This ecumenism has been a continuation or resurgence of the old denominationalism. It has not sufficiently addressed the new denominationalism or the radical diversity that sacralizes the landscape with minarets, Zen centers, and Theravada temples.

There were those, however, who saw in the ecumenical movement a watering down of true Christianity. They understood this cooperation and doctrinal discussion as the work of Satan, encouraging Christians to give in to the modern world and to reinterpret their faith in ways that the world would find congenial. Ecumenism that sought to address diversity by cooperation was, for them, the mark of the Beast, the progeny of liberalism and the Social Gospel. Many who opposed ecumenism retreated from the denominations that supported the ecumenical movement and began to reassert "the faith once delivered to the saints." Their dissent became the basis for a further proliferation of religious diversity. New denominations were born out of the refusal to compromise with what they considered a "watering down of the Gospel."

J. Gresham Machen, who graduated from Princeton Theological Seminary and was further educated in Germany, was a professor of the New Testament at Princeton for more than twenty years in the early twentieth century. His Presbyterian denomination provided significant leadership to the ecumenical movement. Machen became convinced that the principles of the movement were in conflict with his understanding of Christianity. In 1923 he published *Christianity and Liberalism*, a book that juxtaposed the two ingredients of his title. One was either a Christian or a liberal ecumenist. The two alternatives were separate and distinct. Machen took the separatist option, broke with his denomination, and became the intellectual force behind the formation of a new denomination. His words reveal the manner in which his point of view is in conflict with the old denominational position.

Admitting that scientific objections may rise against the particularities of the Christian religion—against the Christian doctrines of the person of Christ, and of redemption through His death and resurrection—the liberal theologian seeks to rescue certain of the general principles of religion, of which these particularities are thought to be mere temporary symbols and these general principles he regards as constituting "the essence of Christianity."[11]

The refusal to compromise with the notion of "general principles" becomes, in the American constitutional context of "no establishment" and "free exercise," a basis for the increase of religious diversity in accordance with the denominational model.

The history of the Amish in America also illustrates this observation. The Old Order Amish, as they are called in Lancaster County, Pennsylvania, and elsewhere, are a religious society that bases its continued existence upon a strict dualism as expressed in the Schleitheim Confession of 1527.

> Now there is nothing else in the world
> And among all creatures
> Than good and evil,
> Faith and unfaith,
> Darkness and light,
> World and those who are outside the world,
> Temples of God those of the idols,
> Christ and Behal,
> And none may have part in the other.[12]

In Amish thought, this dualism means exactly what it says: There are those in the world who are children of the good, faith, and light; they are the temples of God among temples of God-impersonators who represent evil, darkness, and unfaith. I translate the words "gläubig und ungläubig" as "faith and unfaith" rather than "belief and unbelief" because the latter connote assent to certain propositions, whereas "faith and unfaith" are truer to the quality of meaning contained in the Confession and subscribed to by the Amish. "Faith and unfaith" refer to a trusting relationship, the notion that all is well even in the midst of evidence to the contrary. The Amish trust in the good, the God who calls them into being. They are in covenant with one another as they are in covenant with this God. They do not exist as individuals, or as a collectivity of individuals, but as those dedicated to a community of good that gives them life.

The Amish cannot compromise with the world. There is no compromise. They exist as a denomination in a resurgent confessional sense rather than in the old sense because they once were part of the Swiss Brethren, who Jakob Ammann and his followers thought were compromising with the world. The seventeenth- and early eighteenth-century European religious movement known as Pietism had exerted a profound influence upon much of Protestantism and the Anabaptist traditions. Pietism had its counterparts in Judaism, with the emergence of Hasidism, and in Roman Catholicism as Quietism.

Pietism was concerned with renewing the lifeless spirit of the Lutheran and Reformed Churches. It sought to establish conventicles (in England, "classes") of those who sought common experience, prayer, and Biblical spirituality. It stressed virtuous life and practice and tended to be un-mindful of doctrinal differences, ecclesiastical order, and the "middle way" of Lutherans and Reformed who, as Leo Schelbert puts it, "advo-cated a . . . balance between charisma and authority, true faith and spiri-tual experience, obedience to given rules and free-flowing devotion."[13] Pietism influenced the Mennonites and Swiss Brethren, as well as Lutherans and Reformed. Ammann did not like what was happening be-cause Pietism was shaping a tradition of "common essentials" that repre-sented compromise. And, as Schelbert informs us, Ammann was opposed to the individualistic, experiential, innovative, ecumenical, and essentially monist ideas behind Pietism. His uncompromising position led to the sep-aration of the Amish from the Swiss Brethren and Mennonites in 1693.[14]

The Amish are a denomination that exists on the basis of dualistic, un-compromising, and communal characteristics. Schelbert wrote: "When Jakob Ammann and his followers adopted uniform dress, regulated the width of men's hats, and demanded that beards remain untrimmed and hooks and eyes replace buttons, they were not obsessed with trifling exter-nals; they hoped that by such daily tests of obedience the *Gemein* [commu-nity] would remain dedicated to paying attention in all ways only 'to the lips of Christ' as spoken in Holy Writ."[15] And so the Amish exist in America today, from our perspective making a vital contribution to religious diver-sity, one determined by dualism, separation, and failure to compromise.

The denomination has had an interesting history. It has always been both a response to diversity and a facilitator of it. The history of denomi-nationalism reveals a struggle to make diversity work, to separate from its compromising conditions, and to correct its errors. There have been many forms of denominationalism. Whatever its value has been in the past, it falls short of pluralism, the religious perspective of acceptance that is enriched by unity and diversity.

Notes

1. T. S. Eliot, *Christianity and Culture* (New York: Harcourt Brace & Company, 1967), p. 139.

2. Sidney E. Mead, *The Lively Experiment* (New York: Harper & Row, 1963), p. 103.

3. Quoted in Winthrop S. Hudson, *American Protestantism* (Chicago: University of Chicago Press, 1961), p. 42.

4. Quoted in Hudson, p. 33.

5. Quoted in Hudson, p. 46.

6. Edwin S. Gaustad, *Dissent in American Religion* (Chicago: University of Chicago Press, 1973).

7. Cf. John R. Bodo, *The Protestant Clergy and Public Issues, 1812–1848* (Princeton: Princeton University Press, 1954).

8. Cf. Whitney Cross, *The Burned Over District* (Ithaca: Cornell University Press, 1950).

9. Edwin S. Gaustad, *A Documentary History of Religion in America,* vol. 1 (Grand Rapids, MI: Wm. B. Eerdmans, 1982), p. 352.

10. Robert Bellah et al., *Habits of the Heart* (New York: Harper & Row, 1985), esp. chap. 6.

11. J. Gresham Machen, quoted in Gaustad, *Documentary History,* vol. 2, 2nd ed. (1993), p. 395.

12. Leo Schelbert, "Pietism Rejected: A Reinterpretation of Amish Origins," in *America and the Germans,* ed. Frank Trommler and Joseph McVeigh (Philadelphia: University of Pennsylvania Press, 1985), p. 122.

13. Ibid., p. 121.

14. Ibid., p. 123.

15. Ibid., p. 124.

4
Diversity and the Public Order: The Way of Civil Religion

The attempt to make religious and cultural diversity amenable to the common good has led to the adoption of many religious positions. Conquest and conversion are still adopted as responses to the otherness that is both attractive and repellent. In the social circumstances of history, Americans have devised institutions whose very existence is a testimony to their struggle to find ways to transcend differences or eliminate them. Denominationalism has been a unique manifestation of this institutional response. Conquest, conversion, and denominationalism are all models of response to religious diversity. In all of these responses there resides a religious motivation—an effort to express the ultimate order and meaning of existence. Denominationalism expresses attitudes of conquest and conversion as well as the hope for cooperation and the transcendence of conflict. To accept diversity is to acknowledge that there exists a good that is greater than our vision of it.

Nowhere perhaps is the religious acceptance of diversity so important as in relation to the public order of the United States. This has been an acknowledged truth since the beginning of the constitutional republic. "A religious sect," wrote James Madison in 1787, "may degenerate into a political faction in a part of the Confederacy; but the variety of sects dispersed over the entire face of it must secure the national Councils against any danger from that source."[1]

Madison's thinking sought to avoid the mischief of factionalism that would likely become prevalent in a diverse public domain. He had come to the conclusion that factions are unavoidable because the attempt to ban them or to impose common opinions and interests would infringe upon liberty. Madison assumed that the only way to manage diversity is to see that it is dispersed throughout the land. Debates in the Constitutional Convention eventually led to the publication of the First Amendment, the initial clause of which states that "Congress shall make no law respecting an establishment of religion, or prohibiting the free exercise thereof." That clause is not readily interpreted. It exists as a legal principle that must constantly be applied to the setting and circumstances of history. We do not know ideally or abstractly what it means; we always *learn* what it means. Its meaning changes. What is quite evident, however, is that Congress (not the federal state and not the president) must refrain from any legal attempt to establish a religion or some notion of religion. Religions must be free to be or not to be, and in their freedom they will disperse throughout the land and attach no sacred significance to any part of it.

We must remember, however, that Madison revealed another important principle about the place of religion in a republic. The establishment clause, as Leonard Levy reminds us, depoliticizes religion. It "separates government and religion so that we can maintain civility between believers and unbelievers as well as among the several hundred denominations, sects, and cults that thrive in our nation, all sharing the commitment to liberty and equality that cements us together."[2] The clause may depoliticize religion, but it does not "deculturize" it as long as liberty and equality are shared commitments that cement Americans together. Liberty and equality are aspects of the religious acceptance of a good that is not *possessed* by any religion. Madison's dispersal principle exists in relation to his theory regarding religion that holds that liberty and equality are essential aspects of the religious foundations of a civil society.

Madison held that the duty owed by his fellow citizens to the Creator and the manner of carrying this duty out were matters of reason and conviction that were best left to each citizen. The individual must attend to this duty before becoming a responsible member of civil society. "Before any man can be considered as a member of Civil Society, he must be considered as a subject of the Governor of the Universe: and if a member of Civil Society, who enters into any subordinate association, must always do it with a reservation of his duty to the General Authority; much more must every man who becomes a member of any particular Civil Society, do it with a saving of his allegiance to the Universal Sovereign."[3]

Madison's idea may be unnecessarily privatistic and individualistic. That, of course, is in keeping with the assumptions of the American Enlightenment and of modernism, in both its Reformational and more philosophical forms. The individualism of this point of view extends the boundaries of diversity while at the same time recognizing the need for religious responsibility in relation to the public order. According to Madison, civil society cannot exist unless individuals attend to the duty they owe to the Creator, the Universal Sovereign. Congress must not interfere with religions that help people nurture their private religious responsibilities; and "in matters of Religion, no mans right is abridged by the institution of Civil Society and that Religion is wholly exempt from its cognizance."[4] The majority must *in no way* infringe upon the rights of a minority.

The ideas of the Constitution's framers were strongly affected by the diversity of American religion. A solution to the dilemma of diversity was to place religious responsibility on the individual. It was assumed that if religions were left to themselves, they would contribute to civil society by stabilizing the social order and reminding individuals of their religious duties. A principle similar to the concept of pluralism is at work here, because the religious needs of civil society are not denied or rejected. Instead, it becomes religiously important to transcend differences in order to ensure the uncoerced observance of religious responsibilities. Although no legal or political establishment is possible, a religious and cultural establishment may be implicit in this understanding. The basic assumption behind Madison's "Civil Society" is that religious responsibility is essential to the social order, that religions may have a share in nurturing that responsibility, and that adherents of particular religions must in some sense transcend their traditional or denominational loyalties.

The way is open for a consideration of what some thinkers have called American civil religion.[5] But first it may be necessary to examine the significance of the First Amendment in relation to these ideas. Thomas Jefferson spoke of a "wall of separation between church and State."[6] Obviously, this is not the language of the First Amendment; it is Jefferson's attempt to interpret the meaning of the First Amendment's language. According to Jefferson's thinking, no existing denomination, often referred to as a "church," could impose itself upon the public domain represented by the government. No combination of denominations, thinking of themselves as "the church," could expect to affect directly the workings of government. For Jefferson there was a "wall" that separated the forms of civil and ecclesiastical governance. But Jefferson's use of the metaphor of the wall does not give absolute status to the metaphor. Nor is his use of the terms "church" and "State" beyond question. When Americans think of the meaning of the First Amendment, they may prejudice the outcome by using Jefferson's terms.

In 1947, for example, Supreme Court Justice Hugo Black provided a classic example of this confusion in his statement of interpretation in the case of *Everson v. Board of Education:*

> The "establishment of religion" clause of the First Amendment means at least this: Neither a state nor the Federal Government can set up a church. Neither can pass laws which aid one religion, aid all religions, or prefer one religion over another. . . . No tax . . . can be levied to support any religious activities or institutions, whatever they may be called, or whatever form they may adopt to teach or practice religion. . . . In the words of Jefferson, the clause against es-

tablishment of religion by law was intended to erect "a wall of separation between church and State."[7]

Note here the confusing interchangeable use of the words "religion" and "church." These words have separate and different origins; they do not mean the same thing. Because there is no consistency of language in Black's statement, a basic misunderstanding of the nature of religion is advocated. The Amendment clause refers to the establishment of "religion." In his first level of interpretation, Justice Black transposes the word "religion" to inform us that the "clause" means that no government "can set up a *church*." He further tells us that there can be no legal aid to one "religion" or to all "religions" and that no preference can be given to "one religion over another." We are then told that there can be no governmental financial support for any *religious* activities *or institutions;* indeed, no taxes are to be used to enhance any agency or activity that *touches or practices* "religion." The argument closes by reminding us that prohibiting Congress from engaging in the establishment of *religion* is equivalent to erecting a wall of separation between *church* and state.

The point is that a confusion of language makes for a confusion of understanding and that the interpretative statement made by Justice Black requires further careful interpretation. By equating the terms "religion" and "church," the statement reveals its author's inability to move beyond the cultural circumstances in which "religion" means "church," denomination, or institution. But what happens when we begin to understand that religion can take cultural and social forms other than churches, denominations, and the usual institutions? It then becomes nothing short of ridiculous to say that the government can provide no support for the teaching or practice of religion *of any sort.* Can the nation reject those religious ideas and practices that are part of its own fundamental character? Can it oppose the convictions and ritual enactments that make it a nation? If America is a nation "conceived in liberty, and dedicated to the proposition that all men are created equal," then Americans will seek to incarnate these beliefs with stories and addresses and to develop festivals and ritual occasions giving them full expression. However, it should also be noted that this individualistic, Protestant, Enlightenment way of defining and expressing religion may infringe upon the rights of traditional peoples for whom religion signifies their cultural relation to particular sacred places in the landscape.

Americans may establish no religion in its churchly, denominational, or institutional forms. But Americans have never, at least until recently, been able to avoid advocating the religion that is the unique spiritual entity of their nation, or that represents their attempt to find a sense of order and meaning that enables the *acceptance* of diversity (pluralism). As the

English journalist G. K. Chesterton was to observe early in the twentieth century, America was "a nation with the soul of a church." It was a nation that gave profound spiritual expression to the idea that it could take many diverse peoples and religions and make them one.

Alexis de Tocqueville was an astute observer of the religious character of this unique new republic. "In the United States," he wrote in his two-volume *Democracy in America,* "no religious doctrine displays the slightest hostility to democratic and republican institutions. The clergy of *all the different sects* there hold the same language; their opinions are in agreement with the laws, and the human mind flows onwards, so to speak, in one undivided current."[8] But what really astounded Tocqueville was the fact that, without a legal establishment, religion exerted a greater influence over public life than it did in European nations where religion enjoyed full legal establishment. Why? "In the United States the sovereign authority is religious, and consequently hypocrisy must be common; but there is no country in the world where the Christian religion retains a greater influence over the souls of men than in America; and there can be no greater proof of its utility and of its conformity to human nature than that its influence is powerfully felt over the most enlightened and free nation of the earth."[9] What Tocqueville was observing was the manner in which a cultural establishment of religion had taken place where no church or denomination (or totality of denominations) enjoyed legal priority.

"Our sister States of Pennsylvania and New York," noted Thomas Jefferson already in 1782, "have long subsisted without any establishment at all. The experiment was new and doubtful when they made it. It has *answered beyond conception.* They flourish infinitely. *Religion is well supported; of various kinds,* indeed, but *all good enough;* all *sufficient to preserve peace and order;* . . . Let us give this experiment fair play" (italics mine). Jefferson's notion of the "good enough" character of legally unestablished denominations reminds us that these religious institutions were indeed good for something, that they were well supported, diverse, *and performed an essential role.* They were "good enough" without legal establishment to make a fundamental contribution to the "peace and order" of American society. *Legally* unestablished denominations assisted in the fashioning of a *cultural* establishment of those values and ideas essential to the acceptance of diversity and to the cohesiveness and unity of the emerging republic.

This cultural establishment represented the fashioning of a kind of public constitution, an American commonality, a basic unity that made possible a document like the Constitution of the United States of America. Without this public "constitution" it may not have been possible for the Constitution framing the American government to have become effective. But what about this "constitution," this cultural establishment? Was it merely something for scholars to debate? Leonard Levy, a foremost constitutional historian, seems not to understand the principle of a cultural establishment or of a popular "constitution" when he writes that "religion flourishes best when left to private voluntary support in a free society."[10] The "free society" of the new constitutional republic was not an aggregate or collectivity of individuals; it was an organic reality, a constituted people nurtured by common values and ideas preserved by institutions that did their work well enough even though they were not legally established.

There was indeed a kind of "civil" religion at work. Critics of the notion of civil religion are often confused by the false assumption that religion must always assume the voluntary, individualistic, institutional form adopted by American denominations. A religion, they assume, must be an entity that an individual can voluntarily join or decide not to join. They have little understanding of religion as organic, communal, and spatially related—the customs of a people in relation to a special, sacred place. One does not, for example, *join* the Hopi or the Navajo; these peoples do not practice their religions privately, apart from the greater sense of community and ethnicity. In a sense, during much of the sweep of colonial American history, there existed a religious constitution that has made the diverse civilization into a people of common values. Critics of American "civil religion" have been skeptical of Bellah's use of this term, suggesting that there is no provision for "joining" the civil religion that he discusses, that there is no regularized dogma or sacerdotal leadership.

A civil religion is like a tribal tradition; it is basically a sacred and organic reality into which one is born. One does not have to subscribe; one just is and does as "this people" does. However, in the case of American civil religion, there are various rituals of initiation that have served to bring people into the tradition. Infant baptism, for example, has been as much an *American* ritual as a Christian sacrament with its attendant theological significance. Parents have as a matter of course had their children baptized without reference to theological meaning. It has become an American thing to do, whether the parents are devout and participating Christians or not. The religious revivals of the nineteenth-century frontier also functioned to initiate individuals into their duties to the "Creator" or the "Universal Sovereign," to ensure that the civil society would be maintained in spite of the "barbarism" and lawlessness of frontier life.

"In the model of the Republic," writes Sidney Mead, "the civil authority [read Constitution] intends that the temple-ists [read denominations] shall curb one another by protecting the right of each continually to tell 'the other that he is not God.'"[11] Mead writes elsewhere of a "theology" of the republic, by which he referred to a constellation of images and ideas that related to the character of the republic itself and that required constant analysis and clarification. "The theology of [the] denominations," he writes, "is different from the theology that legitimates the constitutional and legal structure of their country."[12] This is only true if we agree that rationalistic consistency is not just an element in private judgment but a social possibility as well. These theologies of which Mead speaks are only "different" if we assume that the "theologies" of the denominations make no contribution, and have no responsibility, to the "theology" of the republic.

In the early years of the republic, this relationship was perfectly clear. "Without the common sense of identity, loyalty, purpose provided by civil religion," writes Leroy Rouner,

> the individualism and rationalism of modern pluralistic society would have made democracy dysfunctional, for there would have been no common ground. Civil religion, for example, makes possible the paradox of a "loyal opposition" within a rational government. It is the binding ingredient of pluralistic democracy, holding individuals and institutions to the national community even when their particular political will has not prevailed.[13]

There have been many articulations of this civil religion; accordingly, the term must be used flexibly, and we are under no spell of dictionary determinism. Something of what John Dewey referred to as our "common faith" was at work in civil religion. Dewey said that religion is a particularistic kind of enterprise that distorts the basic religiousness of human beings. A democracy celebrating diversity challenges the particularisms and allows a common faith to be nurtured by democratic education. The common faith, like the civil religion, is an expression of pluralism, the religious assumption that the ultimate order and meaning of existence require the acceptance of diversity. However, unlike Jefferson and civil religion, Dewey destroys the pluralism of his "common faith" by setting it against particular traditions, thereby rejecting genuine diversity. "The positive lesson," he wrote,

> is that religious qualities and values if they are real at all are not bound up with any single item of intellectual assent, not even that of the existence of the God of theism; and that, under existing conditions, the religious function in experience can be emancipated only through surrender of the whole notion of special truths that are religious by their own nature, together with the idea of peculiar avenues of access to such truths.[14]

Pluralism as religion may require the *transcendence* of "special truths that are religious by their own nature." It recognizes, however, that those particular traditions have a right to exist, and that in some sense they point to a truth beyond, or complementary to, their "special truth." This kind of truth is always symbolic, which means that it participates in a truth greater than its own representation or understanding.

J. Paul Williams took up this same theme to suggest that the denominations had failed in their responsibility to the republic.[15] Therefore democracy itself must assume religious proportions and government must see to it that the "democratic ideal as religion" is taught and promulgated. In this scenario, democracy itself becomes the civil religion, a *legally established* religion no less, and quite different from the cultural establishment expressed in the early form of civil religion. Again, by failing to accept the diversity of traditions, Williams suggests a religion of democracy, a kind of civil religion that rejects the ability of particular traditions to participate in the religious order of the common good. Williams's religion is a new religion that, like Joseph Smith's, seeks to avoid diversity by suggesting a new and *separate* religious order instead of a religious truth that affirms the richness of diversity.

Civil religion was initially not the religion *of* the republic, but an organic tradition that represented the constitution of values and ideas originally developed through the presence of Christianity in early American history. Civil religion in its early republican form was the tradition that made the republic possible and found public expression *alongside of,* but *related* to, denominational and institutional religion.

The Shape of Civil Religion

What is civil religion? In what sense is it a religious tradition, and how does it attempt to address the issues of diversity and take us in the direction of pluralism? There is a story to tell that sheds light on the origins of the American people.

A myth is recounted, telling the story of who the American people are, why they came to America, and what they stand for. (Myths, we remember, are not falsehoods, untruths, or misconceptions. They are quite the opposite—they are the imaginative truths by means of which people construct their lives and order their thinking.)

"In the beginning," wrote John Locke, "all the world was America."[16] For Europeans, America was the "Land Promised to the Saints," the last remnant of the Garden of Eden, the world as it was. The myths behind American civil religion communicate that primordial condition; America was before time as we know it, before history. The story includes an event similar to the Exodus. The Declaration of Independence and the War of Independence are the occasion of America's emancipation and America's right to claim the title of "Promised Land" in order to bring into being a new people, not like the contentious people of the European captivity. "Four score and seven years ago," said Abraham Lincoln in the Gettysburg Address, "our fathers brought forth on this continent a new nation." It was a new nation, according to Lincoln, that was seeking to forge a union out of a multiplicity of peoples and regions, all of whom had found it difficult to contemplate their otherness. The myth develops variations, but continues to tell the story of who the Americans are as a people and what the meaning of life is for them.

But it is not only myths that arise. Myths give life to symbols, to legends about special people, places, and events that embody the story. George Washington becomes the father of the country, a figure whose courage, dedication, and honor symbolize what America stands for. What Americans say and think about Washington reveals a great deal about the American character. Washington's role as symbol and saint of civil religion is certainly as important as the historical role he played. In the nineteenth century the legends of Daniel Boone and Davy Crockett reveal a different facet of the American myth; and more mythic figures such as Mike Fink and Paul Bunyan demonstrate the ability of archetypal myths to generate derivatives and blend with legendary elements.

In these myths and legends we can discern the theories, doctrines, and ideas that are basic to the civil tradition. We know that Americans believe in equality; for example, that they constitute a leveling society in which citizenship is valued for its ingenuity, native intelligence, effort, and private initiative. Davy Crockett is a frontier figure, a paradigmatic American, who is smarter and more skilled than any refined and formally educated easterner.

But there are also written texts, like sacred scriptures, that embody and preserve those teachings that construct the American "world" with its sense of what is ultimately meaningful. There are, for example, the Declaration of Independence and the Constitution. We may remember that Martin Luther King Jr., used the Declaration as a homiletic text in the same way that he might have used material from the New Testament. The rhetorical pattern of the "I Have a Dream" speech finds its home in the language of the Declaration and in the sermonic style of African American Baptist churches. The speech has great potential to join the canon of American scriptures; there is perhaps no finer example of the scriptural power of the Declaration than King's address. Yet we remember also that the canonical status of the Declaration found its full measure of authority in Abraham Lincoln's famous address at the national cemetery in Gettysburg, Pennsylvania, in 1865.[17]

There are, of course, lesser documents that are reminiscent of the sacred truth that is at the heart of the American experiment. John Winthrop, in his "Model of Christian Charity," a sermon delivered aboard the ship *Arabella* before he and his fellow Puritans disembarked in Massachusetts Bay in 1630, provided sacred images that have shaped American self-understanding ever since. Few American presidents, indeed few national political leaders, have been able to avoid speaking of America as a "city upon a hill," the "eyes of all people upon us." John F. Kennedy's inaugural address in January 1961 will very likely be remembered as a beloved reference, a quoted text in the civil tradition. Lincoln's Gettysburg Address and his second Inaugural address, James Madison's "Memorial and Remonstrance," and Martin Luther King Jr.'s "I Have a Dream" are classic and sacred testimonies that celebrate the sacred significance of American self-understanding.

There are also American saints, those human beings whose lives have become the incarnation of what is most valued in American society. Washington and Lincoln are probably the most exalted of these divine beings. The painting and sculpture that seeks to convey what America thought of Washington frequently represents him among the gods of the Greek pantheon, or as a Christlike figure, ascending into the heavens accompanied by an angelic host. Lincoln is an American Christ. Assassinated on Good Friday, he was a victim, a sacrificial figure who healed the wounds of turbulent and unredeemed diversity. He died so that there might be Union, a unity among diverse peoples who had torn the nation apart for the sake of their inordinate self-interest. Lincoln's blood was shed for his people, sanctifying the very ground that had been saturated with the blood of those thousands who had given their lives for the cause of unity amid diversity. As Catherine Albanese points out, the rebirth of the spirit of the revolution took place when the Marquis de Lafayette visited the United States as an old man in 1824. An eagle was spotted flying over Washington's tomb as Lafayette entered to pay homage to his beloved mentor.

> Then some two years later, the deaths of John Adams and Thomas Jefferson *on the Fourth of July,* 1826, awed and impressed Americans. The two had died hours apart on the fiftieth anniversary of the signing of the Declaration of Independence. Once more, Americans believed they had a sign from God. . . . Again in the following decade, when the physical remains of George Washington were placed in a new marble coffin, Americans learned that his body was physically nearly intact (he had died in 1799). No odor offended those present; the broad temples and chest were there; and one member of the party quickly laid his hand on Washington's head. . . . The wholeness of Washington's body seemed a sign of the wholeness of America grounded on its past.[18]

We are not dealing with some far-fetched and novel understanding of religion when we call attention to the myths, scriptures, and saints that are an intrinsic aspect of American self-understanding. These phenomena help Americans to know when and where time begins. It begins with divinely guided "discoveries" by Europeans. It begins with a revolution in the behavior and attitudes of human beings who know that they are a new people. The ultimate truths of American self-understanding must be celebrated; they must be ritually expressed.

And so there are those special days and observances like Memorial Day, the birthdays of Washington and Lincoln, the Fourth of July, and Thanksgiving, all of which are occasions for performing, acting out, what it meant to belong to America, the newly chosen Israel. There have been a considerable number of lesser holy days in the civil sacred calendar, some that have all but disappeared, others that have been sentimentalized and commercialized to the point where their sacred significance has been lost. Some, like Mother's Day, are basically "Hallmark" days, although they retain a kind of feasting and gift-giving character that has always had a religious significance. Americans remember mother because she has made them who they are as Americans; she is God's gift of love, stability, and morality in a world that is unsure and uncaring. She stands for America, because America cares.

It is interesting, in this connection, to contemplate the fate of the holidays commemorating Washington's and Lincoln's birthdays. These two holidays have been compressed into Presidents' Day, and there is basically nothing to celebrate, nothing to honor or remember. Holidays like Presidents' Day are essentially concessions to the consumer culture and the tourism industry, both of which thrive on self-indulgence. Holiday weekends on our recreational rivers and lakes are facilitated by the boats that we must buy. Our visits to mountains and deserts are made more exciting by the all-terrain vehicles that are symptomatic of our failure to live with silence, solitude, and the creative imagination. Nothing is honored, nothing is remembered. But there were once holy days in the civil calendar. My public school teachers were good storytellers. In school they related the myths and the legends to us. They told us that "all men were created equal." They told the girls as well as the boys. And we all knew that to belong to "this people America" is to know something about equality. We obviously didn't know all we needed to know. We never do. But then, anything really meaningful has more truth to it than we can understand at any given time. That's the way with equality. In school we made pictures of Washington and Lincoln—on their birthdays. We always had cherries, candy cherries on green wire stems, by which to remember Washington. So later I learned that that story about young Washington chopping down a cherry tree was probably not true. *But it was true;* I know that now. It *was true* because our people told it that way. It was true because our grandfather wanted us to be truthful. He knew that if we forgot truth we would have nothing to tell, that we would never discover how untruthfully we act when we exclude someone from the story of equality. I didn't know anything about a "civil religion" when I was a boy. We never used the word "religion" at all. We just went to Sunday School and attended church services. We listened to our teachers talk about the

Fourth of July and Thanksgiving. We went to the cemeteries on Memorial Day and heard speeches, listened to prayers, and stood by as the band played "The Battle Hymn of the Republic," "Faith of Our Fathers," "Rock of Ages," and "My Country 'Tis of Thee." We imagined Washington and pictured Lincoln in his log house. It was all together, one thing—the "civil religion" and whatever else you did in church and at home to keep the world in some kind of meaningful order.

This, then, is what we mean by civil religion. It is that cluster of ideas and convictions, the special practices, and the sense of peoplehood that belong to America. This symbolic cluster appeared in the sky over the nation, drawing its light from the many denominations of Christianity and the heritage of Judaism. That's the way it was at first; the civil religion, after all, did not emerge from a vacuum. There already existed a many-faceted world of ideas and practices that had to be reconciled to each other in a land with no legal establishment. The civil religion has been difficult for many people to recognize and to accept because it has no church buildings and keeps no membership statistics, but also because so many of its cherished symbols resemble those of Christianity or Reform Judaism. But the civil religion has always been there, call it what you will. And it once had a great deal to do with America's pilgrimage on the way to pluralism.

A real issue facing Americans in their radically diverse circumstances is whether any kind of "sacred canopy" is possible or even necessary. Can Americans exist in a state of "raw" diversity? Is there a public dimension to their existence that is shared beyond religious and cultural enclaves? It seems impossible to avoid the sacred necessity of what civil religion represents and the fact that Americans do share a public existence. Perhaps a people that has no regard for unity in its diversity, a unity that it has some responsibility for nurturing, some stake in expressing and celebrating, will fall victim to external religious forces over which it has no control. There are signs that the technological and corporate world is fashioning just such a structure of external religiosity. The extent to which Americans' values and ideas are determined by the media, by technology, and by the business component of society is indicative of religiousness at work. Perhaps this religiousness will overcome America's diversity without achieving a real pluralism that accepts diversity and encourages a commitment to a common good that is nurtured by manyness—by the multiplicity of those who dwell within and among.

Notes

1. James Madison, "The Federalist, No. 10," in *American Ground*, ed. Robert H. Fossum and John K. Roth (New York: Paragon House, 1988), p. 64.

2. Leonard Levy, *The Establishment Clause* (New York: Macmillan, 1986), p. ix.

3. James Madison, "Memorial and Remonstrance," in Edwin S. Gaustad, *A Documentary History of Religion in America*, vol. 1 (Grand Rapids, MI: Wm. B. Eerdmans, 1982), p. 263.

4. Ibid.

5. See Robert N. Bellah, "Civil Religion in America," *Daedalus* 117, no. 3 (Winter 1967).

6. Levy, pp. 181–182.

7. Quoted in ibid., pp. 123–124.

8. Alexis Comte de Tocqueville, *Democracy in America*, vol. 1 (New York: Vintage Books, 1960), pp. 312–313.

9. Ibid., p. 314.

10. Levy, p. xii.

11. Sidney E. Mead, *The Nation with the Soul of a Church* (New York: Harper & Row, 1975), p. 10.

12. Ibid., p. 125.

13. Leroy S. Rouner, *To Be at Home* (Boston: Beacon Press, 1991), p. 3.

14. John Dewey, *A Common Faith* (New Haven: Yale University Press), pp. 32–33.

15. J. Paul Williams, *What Americans Believe and How They Worship* (New York: Harper & Row, 1962), p. 371.

16. John Locke, *The Second Treatise of Government*, 49, 1.

17. Cf. Gary Wills, *Inventing America* (Garden City, NY: Doubleday, 1978).

18. Catherine L. Albanese, *America: Religions and Religion* (Belmont, CA: Wadsworth Publishing, 1981), pp. 301–302.

5

Race, Gender,
and Ethnicity

In a culture of disestablishment and civil religion, there is no curtailment of the religious impulse. Every instance of injustice, every occasion of idealism and resistance to homogeneity, every new insight and discovery can give rise to a new religious movement. Many social and cultural movements with no apparent or obvious use of religious language are nevertheless expressive of the religious inclination to give shape to a sense of ultimate order and meaning. When traditional and readily accepted forms of religion have eroded, the impulse seeks new forms. The diversity of denominational religion may still be a factor in American culture, as traditions from Asia and the Middle East make their adjustments to the denominational and institutional nature of American religion. Jews, Roman Catholics, Eastern Orthodox Christians, Muslims, and Buddhists have adapted to the denominational character of American culture. The priest in a Buddhist temple acts very much like the pastor of a Protestant church; he tries to shape his temple into a congregation of those who compete for institutional success in the marketplace culture.

Ben Winton, writing about the contemporary search for faith and suitable places of worship, quotes the rector of the All Saints Episcopal Church in Phoenix, Arizona, as follows: "People shop for churches like they shop for a lot of things." Apparently the traditional loyalties are no longer valid in the great diversity of American religion. Non-Muslims show up for prayers in Arizona's mosques. The imam of Al-Islam Mosque insists that people seek openly: "They are searching for the same thing that all are searching for—truth and peace. . . . The Koran lets you know that peace is the home of understanding."[1] "Search" is a key term in understanding the nature of contemporary religions and cultural life. In traditional societies, the individual does not "search," but belongs; and religious life has to do with being at home among the many images, symbols, stories, and rituals that shape one's perception of the world. "Search" in traditional society gives rise to the mystic or the charismatic figure who has recovered some element from the depths of the tradition. At the threshold of twenty-first-century America, "search" is a derivative of diversity and modernity. And, although "search" may lead the individual in the direction of any one of a number of institutions that sacralize the landscape, it also leads to a syncretistic form of behavior in which the searcher does not associate as a member of any particular institution. Instead, one adopts a form of Hindu yoga for meditation, goes to occasional prayer group meetings, reads the Bible regularly, goes to a Native American sweat lodge, and privately contemplates the ideas of St. John of the Cross. This behavioral pattern is not necessarily to be associated with the so-called New Age religiousness. It is simply the result of the new diversity in American religion.

As has been said, however, religious diversity also increases with the emergence of certain forms of cultural consciousness that are emancipated in the course of the breakdown of traditional and modern society. Race, gender, and ethnicity are three of these cultural conventions that contribute to diversity while also enjoying liberation as a result of the rising sense of pluralism.

One of the characteristics of modernity and of modern religion has been the tendency toward the total manipulation of society, or total imperialism. Modern science, technology, and business function by a principle of control; the world, its resources, and its ideas must be manipulated for the sake of success and progress. Differences can only be permitted if they have no public effect and do not interfere with the agenda of Western science, technology, and commerce. A computerized society cannot permit computer illiteracy. There must be no alternative methods or truths. People of earlier cultures are ignorant, and those who linger on the outskirts of modern Western civilization must be enlightened; they must be taught the new ways. Newer is always truer, in this way of thinking; "Don't stop progress" is the corollary admonition.

The modern mind tolerates no magic, no superstition, no "primitive" notions. Instead of asking what magic is, what it means to the people, or whether there is a legitimate epistemological reality being expressed, the modern mind must sweep it into the dark night of the past. Obviously the same assumptions apply to what is called superstition. There is no regard for the fact that superstition may be a significant element in the ordering of a meaningful and dynamic life. Such practices as magic and superstition admit too much that is unmanageable into the intellectual and scientific enterprise. Modern thinking also invests the term "primitive" with a negative connotation. Instead of regarding "primitive" as being merely earlier in time or of a different place, we assume that it is cruder and inferior. The modern mind finds it difficult to accept the fact that a traditional society, living for example in the Amazonian backcountry, may be comprised of people who are as intelligent as those who live in late-twentieth-century America. It is almost impossible for the modern mind to regard the Amazonian way of thinking and acting as being sophisticated in its own right. These South American peoples, like most traditional peoples, regard themselves as elements in a cosmic community. Westerners, on the other hand, believe that traditional peoples stand in the way of enterprise. Their differences must be disregarded so that modern society can justify the "purchase" of their world, the violation of its sacredness, and the utilization of its resources toward predetermined ends.

However, it is becoming increasingly evident that many forms of resistance to the sanctity of modernism have arisen. The problem is that modernity finds its fullest expression in the technocorporate world. Therefore the power lies with modernity; this gives rise to apocalyptic theories that posit some kind of ultimate conflagration, an Armageddon matching the forces of modernity against those of postmodern protest.

The forms of resistance to modernity were probably first evident during the years 1914 to 1918, when it was observed by some that there were flaws in the expectations of modern optimists. Apparently all was not well with the homogenization process that had sought to build a utopian society and bring it to progressive consummation by the turn of the twentieth century. T. S. Eliot gave profound voice to postmodern sentiment in poems like "The Waste Land" and "The Hollow Men," published in 1922 and 1925, respectively. F. Scott Fitzgerald's novel *The Great Gatsby* offered a sobering word of caution to the sentimentality of modernistic faith. The Great Depression of the 1920s and early 1930s sounded another note of warning, although the prevailing American optimism tended to assume that a devastating world war and a depression were only temporary setbacks. Modernism, after all, had been accompanied by a deep faith and loyalty to technical reason. The modernistic mind, in its fidelity to the human right to abstract itself from its world and proceed to the creation of other worlds, addresses existence as a problem. A problem is an abstraction, of course; a problem seeks to derive manageable and manipulatable elements from any context it observes. A problem can be "solved" by marshaling skills and experience—the resources of technical reason. If something is "wrong" or "not working as expected," the modern mind assumes that it can be reduced to a "problem" and then fixed.

Problem definition and problem solution are part of the faith of modernism and its devotion to technical reason. Therefore, in the thinking of a modernistic culture, all sobering events are only temporary setbacks. Tomorrow we'll fix it up, make everything right, and be back on track, on the road to utopia. The "problem" is that life is not a "problem," except in modernistic faith. Life is a story to be told and lived with ongoing, creative attention to its unexpected episodes. After the Depression came the Hitlerian and other fascist juggernauts, the Holocaust, World War II, the threat of nuclear devastation, the Cold War, and the wars in Korea and

Southeast Asia. The great postmodern convulsion of the 1960s was a powerful protest against modernity. The African American civil rights struggle accompanied the 1960s revolution and provided a rhetoric for understanding what had been happening. America had been the hospitable milieu in which modernism had gained its status and support. There could be no impediments to the success of the modern agenda. Anything that stood in the way had to be pushed aside. Differences in color, sexuality, religion, and culture had to be ignored, or bleached, or suppressed. They had to be denied any power of their own choosing.

The 1960s was a watershed decade because of the eruptions of postmodern protest and the diversification of American religion, a process that took issues of race, gender, and ethnicity out of traditional religious forms and made them religious concerns in their own right.[2] The values thought to be essential to the development of modern civilization were questioned because they existed in hypocrisy, according to the reformers. According to the revolutionaries, wars, depressions, genocide, and environmental waste all occurred within the context of a society that advocated a morality of truth, honesty, and love for one's neighbor. This same society promoted devotion to monogamous marriage, lifetime fidelity, restraint, and premarital chastity in an era of increasing unfaithfulness and divorce. The modern world, in both its secular and traditionally religious manifestations, had succeeded only in advancing hypocrisy and in manipulating people to detrimental ends; it professed a morality of love while functioning by a morality of power. Modernity made war; the reformers countered with "Make love, not war." There was talk of a "new morality" and a call for the reform of higher education, which should be made more "relevant" to the times. Students demanded a role in the governance of their universities, and championed the rights of African Americans, other minorities, and women. Nudity became a sign of protest against society's ineffective and hypocritical sense of propriety. Men streaked across public stages and walked across campuses in naked rebellion. Women bared their breasts in open defiance of a code of behavior determined by males. This was "the dawning of the Age of Aquarius," a time of cultural subversion and irreverence, a turning away from all that white American modernism represented.

Race as Protest Against Modernity

According to *Webster's New World Dictionary*, race is "any of the different varieties of mankind, distinguished by form of hair, color of skin and eyes, stature, bodily proportions, etc." It is easy to see that this statement is no definition, if by "definition" we refer to a precise determination of the meaning of a word, a determination that does not lend itself to interpretation and argument. There are certainly varieties of humankind. People have different hair textures and colors. The shades of human skin vary. Hair texture and skin color seem to be the most reliable criteria for "racial" determination. When we move beyond these factors, however, the variables and the exceptions tend to render such determinations quite inadequate. Only when we associate eye color, stature, and (perhaps) bodily proportion with the more identifiable elements (hair texture and skin color) of "racial" determination can we refer with any reliability to eye color, stature, and bodily proportion as racial determinants. After all, brown eyes are found among Caucasians, Africans, and East and South Asians. Stature and bodily proportion appear to have little or no value in race determination, especially in the twentieth century when dietary factors can alter the human form among people in all parts of the globe. Watusis may be tall, but so are basketball players. There are short German Americans as well as short Japanese Americans and Italian Americans.

Even hair texture and skin color are not always effective racial determinants. It is interesting that Webster's definition does not include nasal shape and the size and shape of the skull, unless, of course, those factors are subsumed under "bodily proportion"—in which case we might have preferred a term like "physiognomy." There certainly are varieties of humankind in which skin color, hair texture, and facial contours play a role. Perhaps the dictionary should tell us that "race" is a term used to reckon the differences in skin color, hair texture, and facial contours that are evident among human beings. But would we not have to add more words to make the "working definition" effective? Might we not have to add to the phrase "that are evident among human beings" the qualifying phrase "when we regard them in collective fashion"? Once we decide that differentiating skin color, hair texture, and facial contours are necessary elements in our consideration of people *as a group*, then we may wish to use the word "race" to speak of them.

As the modern world developed its political, religious, and economic agenda, group identity became an important feature of public policy. "Races" had to be created so that certain "others" could be regarded as inferior and subject to the race that the leaders signified for themselves. It is important to acknowledge that the concept of "race" is, in effect, a human creation, a functional affair. The need to "classify," to "reckon," and to "signify" is a function of the modern demand to control data and satisfy utilitarian desires. If there is no classification, then there is no science, no technology, no business. In some sense, classification and signification have become essential to modern society's well-being. They are inevitable to today's way of existence. We would throw up our hands in total frustration and helplessness if we were told that we could not file items away properly.

Modern signification and classification tend to make little distinction between different modes of being in the world. Once it becomes possible to regard the world as outside ourselves or "other" than ourselves, then it all becomes "nature." In whatever form we encounter it, it becomes some-"thing," an object of our thought or manipulation. We speak of human nature even as we speak of the nature of rocks and trees, of wolves and spotted owls. Have we ever wondered whether a wolf is really a wolf? Do wolves regard themselves as wolves? Or do they have no such *self*-regard at all, existing only as members of a pack in the forests and plains? Although these questions can be considered somewhat facetious, they help clarify the classification and signification process.

In psychology laboratories we examine human "nature" in the human mind and wonder what "it" can do and how "it" works. But what about *us*—those who *do* the examination and by their signification affect the results of our projected endeavor? Much modern science, technology, psychology, and sociology are projections—enterprises of a mind that is greater than its parts or its partitioning. They are projections—deciding who we are or what we can do in order to control existence by the partial determination of our minds. Failure to recognize this results in human beings regarded as human "resources." In Native American culture neither the individual nor humans in general determine their existence. The coyote, the badger, and the buffalo have as much to say about their own lives as humans have to say about theirs. All of being shares in the act of signification. If there is any significance to the Christian word "sin" among Native Americans, then it is the alienation in which humans project their own need to control into the living circumstance of being. Sin is submitting to the temptation to signify without regard for what is being signified, without confession, without a ceremonial act of setting things back into an order where all is give-and-take, giving and receiving—reciprocal. Sin is allowing homogenization to occur.

The need to signify and classify creates "race," establishing an identity for others without giving them a share in the signification. People in a position to signify decide which people are "others"—*because* of skin color, hair texture, and facial contours. The dark color, broad noses, and tightly spiraled hair of Africans offer the modernist American an opportunity to do more than notice these features. The shades of brown can be transformed into *niger*, blackness. And once that transformation occurs, the signified people become associated with the fear of darkness and uncertainty. Darkness is the household of evil and must be controlled and suppressed. The signifiers did not ask these dark-skinned people who they were. They *told* them, thereby *making them* in a sense, transforming them into some-*thing*, the fate of which the signifiers have the power to determine.

Is it fair to say that almost all racial designation is racism? Racism is an "ism," an ideology connected to our need to classify and signify. In a 1970 essay, Ralph Ellison wrote:

> Since the beginning of the nation, white Americans have suffered from a deep uncertainty as to who they really are. One of the ways that has been used to simplify the answer has been to seize upon the presence of black Americans and use them as a marker, a symbol of limits, a metaphor for the "outsider." . . . Despite his racial difference and social status, something indisputably American about Negroes not only raised doubts about the white man's value system but aroused the troubling suspicion that whatever else the true American is, he is also somehow black.[3]

Ellison refers to "racial differences," but has to acknowledge that these differences would be insignificant if Americans really knew who they were. When white Americans call attention to something called "race" and focus upon its social and cultural significance, they try to overcome their anxiety about what an American is by implying that they are not required to account for their failure to include people whose skin color and social status are assumed to make them inferior. These others are of a different "race." They are obviously of inferior social status because they are not truly American—they have failed the test of Horatio Alger, the true American. They failed because of their "race."

America is an anomaly. There has always been an identity crisis, as Ellison suggested. Who is an American? In order to be successful in the modernist enterprise, the majority of Americans sought to exclude those who made them uneasy. Yet America from the beginning has been a very diverse culture. And the very notion of America had to do with overcoming the differences that had been stylized and inherited from Europe. Back in the eighteenth century, Hector St. John Crevecoeur certainly did not include Africans in his imaginative creation of America, but he affirmed the image that would ultimately not alter the course of American diversity, as the following quotation suggests: "What then is the American, this new man? . . . He is an American, who, leaving behind him all his ancient prejudices and manners, receives new ones from the new mode of life he has embraced."[4] To be American was somehow to be inclusive, not exclusive. It was to face "the troubling suspicion that whatever else the true American is, he is also somehow black." There is the anomaly. Modern Americans have sought to homogenize the scene so that they could control it and overcome their identity crisis. However, they eventually discover that there are Americans whose skin color is black, and yet who are most definitely Americans. And even though skin color may matter, "race" doesn't, because this is the signification made by Europeans and white Americans who required justification for their projected imperialism and equated their own pigmentation with superiority. People are different "races," they said; not all "races" are of equal intellectual and social status. Modern genetics tends to avoid the term "race" because it is basically an arbitrary reference associated with group or ethnic identity. Both race and ethnicity are pragmatic references, not definitive terms.

Race as Protest for Pluralism

However, the terms do not disappear merely because they are dubious. And they will continue to be used in the foreseeable future. They are important to a consideration of types of religious diversity because the effort to resist the great white flood of modernism has required establishing the legitimate status of race, gender, and ethnicity as separate entities outside the mainstream—surviving the flood, as it were. The diversity that results is a move in the direction of pluralism because it resists the tendency to foreclose and accept a partial diversity that still excludes others. Racial, ethnic, and gender exclusion do not accept diversity as a *good*—a good that must be served because it reflects the ultimate order and meaning of being.

African Americans very early on began to see the need to add "black" churches and other religious institutions that served their specific needs to the already great array of religious bodies active in the United States. They based their contributions to diversity upon claims to their own uniqueness, protesting on behalf of *inclusion* in the diversity of American life and thus taking a step in the direction of pluralism. African Americans began to argue that they were thoroughly American, that they had been in America longer than the majority of European Americans, and had developed to a greater extent the characteristics by which the new "American race" was to be known. Who were these African Americans? They were the *true* Americans. If they stood outside the mainstream, away from the flood, it was because they were in some profound sense superior. This notion of an outsider distinctiveness was to take many forms during the next century.[5]

The power of its affirmation was to be more visible at some times than at others. When the African American civil rights movement began to gather strength during the late 1950s and the 1960s, the symbolic power of racial self-identity became profoundly significant. "Black is beautiful" was a declaration of ultimate meaning. "You *are* somebody" revived the hearts of many whose lives had been spent under a spell of inferiority and a sense of human deficiency. Your soul is on ice, Eldridge Cleaver reminded the perpetrators of the flood; you are not as human as you should be because your soul has been left to languish in its own support of oppression.[6] You have been the technicians of a holocaust. But we shall survive. We shall overcome. Black is power. "The man of Black Power will not rest until the oppressor recognizes him for what he is—man," wrote James Cone. "He further knows that in this campaign for human dignity, freedom is not a gift but a right worth dying for."[7]

What we begin to understand is that although the concept of "race" is a signification originally derived from the need to justify superiority in the modern effort to create a world according to rationalistic and empirical specifications, it also becomes a means to *protest* that imperialism. After the emancipation of slaves in 1863, African Americans increasingly sought to create their own denominations. These creations were partly the result of a continuing paternalism on the part of the white clergy who wanted to help the former slaves develop those institutions that would nurture their Christian values in a culture that had made its peace with the white South. But at the same time African American leaders emerged who wanted to nurture their own sense of the meaning of Christianity. They no longer were satisfied with being dependent wards of a society that by and large thought of them as ignorant, illiterate, and servile. Denominations like the Colored Methodist Episcopal Church in America were organized as a result of the combined motivations of white paternalism in the Methodist Episcopal Church, South (southern Methodism since 1844) and the initiative of former slaves who had been beneficiaries of the work of the latter denominations. The new Colored Methodist Church became an alternative to the northern Methodism that sought to reshape the lives of slaves according to the principles of a Christianity quite unlike that of the South. It was also an alternative to the independent African Methodism that had been established by freed African American slaves in the northern United States early in the nineteenth century.[8]

Many Baptist congregations that gave rise to separate denominations were also established among African Americans. Baptist tradition, with its polity of congregational autonomy and frequently democratic leadership, lent itself to the needs of the generally self-educated former slaves who were touched by the liberation of the Christian Gospel and understood its power as a means of asserting human identity and meaning in the midst of their peculiar circumstances. When we contemplate the variety of institutions that arose as distinctively "black" churches, we are forced to conclude that "race" itself may be interpreted in a diversity of ways.

"Race" has frequently been the basis for the development of black Holiness, Pentecostal, Baptist, and Methodist churches. But it is also the basis for the formation of the Peace Mission Movement of Father Divine (1876–1965) and Daddy Grace's United House of Prayer for All People. It was, of course, a powerful element in the development of the Nation of Islam. Wallace D. Fard, a founder of the Nation of Islam, urged African Americans to consider themselves a black nation that must oppose the "blue-eyed devils." He was echoing some of the notions of a mysterious predecessor, Noble Ali Drew, who had sought to establish a nationalistic connection and origin for African Americans because he believed that God can only be God of *a people, a nation*. Fard's successor, Elijah Muhammad, maintained this same principle of nationalistic religion by advocating the establishment of a separate national territory in North America for African Americans. The cosmogonic myth for the Nation of Islam was Yacub's history, which taught the "racial" superiority of African Americans, who were the *original* humanity; and the revengeful plot of Mr. Yacub, a "big-headed scientist," angry with Allah, "to create upon the earth a devil race—a bleached-out, white race of people."

Gender as Protest for Pluralism

In recent times gender considerations have become a significant element contributing to religious diversity both inside and outside of traditional religious structures and categories. As the social and cultural order constructed by modernity has begun to break down, women have begun to struggle for a sense of identity and meaning beyond the roles observable in the modern history that culminated in the nineteenth and early twentieth centuries. The protests of women contribute to diversity and move American culture in the direction of pluralism. There are many points of view represented in what have been called feminist and "womanist" treatises and movements. They cannot be discussed here, but they are all suggestive of the increasing diversity of American religious life.

In the traditions of the African and Native American peoples, the role of the woman is shaped both by biology and by the organic character of the community. The traditional community is organic; its varied functions relating to food, shelter, procreation, kinship, and governance tend to be egalitarian as part of an accepted organic order. As the charismatic teacher St. Paul informs us in the New Testament, a body (organic entity) has many parts. One part does not exist without the other, yet no part may be confused with another, and every part is important in relation to the whole. The body may be more than the sum of its parts, but there is no body without the parts. The head and the heart (center) of the body may hold some elemental status in relation to the whole, but neither truly exists without the rest of the parts. The question of superiority in an organic model of understanding is a misplaced question. An organic model is completely relational. There may be a chief and a priest in a community, but neither maintains a separate or totalitarian position. They are living symbols of the total reality.

In these societies the woman's place may be as symbolic as that of the chief or medicine man—and at least as fundamental. Her existence may be microcosmic, her existence intrinsic to the metaphysical reality of all that is. She is the birth giver. Her society may look up to a "high God," but this amounts to an appreciative awareness of the fact that the mystery of being is more than we observe in the cycle of birth, death, and rebirth. If the "high God" is male in connotation, it is not necessarily a representation of maleness in the human sociobiological sense, but a recognition of the fact that give-and-take, initiative and response, are mutual forces evident in the course of existence. One does not exist without the other.

Therefore, in the functional order of the society a metaphysical principle is at work. There is no simple sociological or anthropological functionalism. Rather, traditional and organic societies remind us that the religious is prior to the social. Even if we point to "function" and say that religious ideas and practices are the ways a society organizes (functions), the symbolic power of the total order suggests that social function is an expression of the fact that reality itself is social. If *reality* is social, then the religious character of being *gives rise to* the social. It is the religious discernment of ultimate order and meaning that expresses itself in social ordering.

Now the white flood of Americanism has bleached out the religious nature of society; it doesn't fit the need to classify and to signify for manipulative purposes. Modernity cannot handle mystery and symbolism. Like Ahab in Melville's *Moby Dick,* modernity must slay the mystery—the great whale. For modernity, the intellectual life is conquest. For Melville's Ishmael, intellectuality is the contemplation of the mystery itself. The bleaching of sociality represented by much (though by no means *all*) of social science leads to a conquest-minded evaluation of the role of gender among people. The woman's role in an African or Native American society cannot be understood in terms of the standardizing judgments of modernity. In these societies the woman's role is metaphysical, and not determined by manipulated function. If she plows the field, we may not assume, using bleached-out, modernistic notions of equality, that she is unequal to the male and is being used for purposes of male domination. Woman is before *w*oman; and before male and female is Man-Woman. "Then God said, 'Let us make humankind in *our* own image; male and female he created them,'" writes the author of the first chapter of Genesis.

This metaphysical and organic understanding of gender is very important to an understanding of race as well, because the great white flood of American modernity had disrupted the organic order and assigned women and men with significations that support the modern conquest of reality. Women were given a role to play. They were barred from participation in economic and political institutions; rather, they became the vicarious means to justify those questionable qualities that males found themselves expressing as they struggled for political and economic power. Women became the divine preserve, the moral savants who could

redeem the society fashioned by males. Their presence salved the con-
sciences of men. They were often idealized and idolized, but seldom
given much of a share in their own signification.

Many women in Victorian America were pleased with their roles. In
some sense their gender made them superior beings in that context. The
masculine world had grown neglectful of the virtues presumably represented by Jesus. Women were to be the redeemers who would help to reshape and adjust the moral order that was being threatened by modern
capitalistic society. Women embraced the romantic conception of children
as essentially good. The romanticism of the mid-nineteenth century was
partly a response to the patterns of power that were associated with the
rationalism of modernity.

The masculine world was aware of the fact that it was guiltily neglect-
ing some of the moral and aesthetic qualities that were essential to human
experience. Men of power tended to defer those qualities to women even
as they removed women from the institutions of power and decision
making. They assumed, of course, that moral and aesthetic considerations
could not disturb the modernistic agenda. They could justify this modernistic signification of women by convincing themselves that women
were the ideal humans. Horace Bushnell, one of the most important
Protestant theologians of mid-nineteenth-century America, affirmed a
synthesizing notion of maternal and religious principles. Mothers, said
Bushnell, were to "plant the angel in the man, uniting him to all heavenly
goodness by predisposition from itself."[9]

In the same year Catherine Beecher, daughter of Lyman and sister of
Harriet and Henry Ward, suggested that the superior tastes, habits, feel-
ings, and opinions of a mother were especially effective in the "plastic
texture" of children's minds. Henry Harbaugh, theologian, poet, and
liturgist of the German Reformed Church (in America), published his *True
Glory of Woman* in 1858. He said that women must not be idolized as he
claimed was done in the circles of wealth and fashion. Harbaugh was
concerned about the process of idolization. This occurs, he wrote, when
woman is raised "above her true sphere, so that [a man] may worship
himself, and have others worship him in her." Idolization is an affair of
keeping a woman for the public eye. But, said Harbaugh, there is a "true
sphere" for women; there is a truth that can be perverted. "Our earthly
love needs a goddess to concentrate it, and hold it in its place. This goddess a wife may be to a husband, a daughter to a parent, a sister to a
brother, and a betrothed to a lover. But such goddesses are not for public,
but for private worship."[10]

Harbaugh opposed what he referred to as "so-called woman's rights
reforms." They were an attempt to masculinize women, he said. God has
made everything in its place. What Harbaugh failed to understand, of
course, was that the especially feminine goddess he envisioned was very

much the creation of modern man, not God. Nevertheless, in his book Harbaugh set forth the "beautiful life of the Virgin Mary" as the model woman, projecting his romanticism onto the life of the young woman whom history recognizes as the mother of Jesus of Nazareth. For Harbaugh, Mary was model, virgin, fiancée, wife, mother, disciple, and saint. A woman attains her true glory by the "interpretation and radiance of the supernatural and heavenly," not because she lives by precepts and rules. "To urge duties upon such as are not prepared by a pious spirit to change these duties into principles, is to make every attempt to perform duty the compulsory legal service of the slave."[11]

At this point Harbaugh's theology is saved by the doctrine of justification by grace through faith, a doctrine stressed in his Reformation heritage. But he uses that understanding of grace to suggest a model for woman based upon Mary as "receiver," the one who submits, in order that she may be the nurturer of the divine in the life of a human existence threatened by an idolatrous, modern, masculine society.

It is obvious that gender becomes a factor in religious pluralism because women are eventually forced to protest their signification by white paternalistic society with its masculinized modernism. The experiences of women in the antislavery movement and in the revivalism of Charles Grandison Finney gave voice to some doubts about their virgin sainthood and their romanticized roles as nurturers and comforters in the male-oriented and guilt-ridden society. Nancy Hardesty examines the relationship of revivalism and feminism in her book *Your Daughters Shall Prophesy.*[12] The revivalism espoused by men like Finney was part of the democratic movement of the early nineteenth century, a development in democratic religion. The voice of the people that had already been expressed in the Great Awakening of the eighteenth century had been gaining confidence since the turn of the century. When in January 1829 Andrew Jackson opened the White House to the common people who had supported his election, his aristocratic predecessor, John Quincy Adams, refused to attend the ceremonies. The event was highly symbolic. Society was changing for men; it was becoming more egalitarian.

Gradually, women were able to sense their own bondage and claim equality, partly because the most common rhetoric of the day was the language of revivalism. Words create worlds. Rhetoric is a means of creating and sustaining worlds of meaning and action. The language of evangelists like Finney gave shape to concepts of human perfectibility and the importance of experience over status, leadership as skillfulness and effectiveness, and the practicality of one's religious experience. The women who became associated with the revivalistic movement learned this rhetoric of religious equality and soon translated it into their own religious and social experience. Many women began praying aloud in mixed assemblies, an unheard-of practice that Finney's supporters would not oppose.

The movement quickly proved hospitable to the needs of many women, such as the Grimké sisters, Angelina and Sarah. The revivalists early on became exponents of the antislavery struggle. After being trained by Theodore Dwight Weld and Henry Stanton, the Grimkés began to hold abolitionist meetings for women. "Men infiltrated the meetings," writes Hardesty, "and suddenly, without design [the women] found themselves addressing 'promiscuous assemblies.'" Responding to accusations about the unseemliness of this behavior, the Grimkés "felt they must defend their rights as women or they would lose their right to speak for the slave."[13] The public struggle for women's rights was under way. Lucretia Mott and even the more skeptical Elizabeth Cady Stanton had links to the revivalist movement, which gave voice to the changing status of women even before the movement managed to articulate theoretical support for women's emancipation. Stanton and Susan B. Anthony, in their *History of Woman Suffrage*, gave little credit to the women within revivalism who had struggled as practitioners and exponents of women's rights. Oberlin College in Ohio, founded in 1834 as a training institute for abolitionism, was the first college to admit women on a par with men. Oberlin and Lane Theological Seminary were under the direction of Finney and Asa Mahan, both leaders of abolitionism and evangelical revivalism. At the heart of these movements was a nineteenth-century concern for the possibilities of human perfection. There were a variety of interpretations of perfection, but for our purposes it is enough to point out that the attempt to reform society was accompanied by the idea that human *will* could be changed and directed toward a greater realization of human equality than had previously been possible.

"At least the Methodist formulation of Christian Perfection," writes Nancy Hardesty, "clearly empowered women. Almost everyone who explored the teaching at all read the testimonies of Hester Ann Rogers, Mary Bosanquet Fletcher, Madame Guyon, and others. And the leading Methodist exponent of the concept in mid-century America and the British Isles was Phoebe Palmer."[14] More traditionally minded Christians like Henry Harbaugh were ill at ease with the "so-called woman's rights reforms" that found expression among Finneyites and the Holiness movement of Phoebe Palmer. Harbaugh sought to protect the "true order" of God's creation by his appeal to the model of the Virgin Mary. Yet his understanding of the Virgin Mary was derived from the modernist need to control the political and economic process. Revivalism itself, opposed by churchmen like Harbaugh, may be understood as yet another form of modernist claims for equality. Yet it spawned a movement that undermined the white masculine order of the rest of modernity.

Gender became a factor in the culture of American pluralism by virtue of the struggle of women for a right to their own signification. This struggle moved through many stages and has probably not yet reached its objectives as the twentieth century comes to an end. Since the 1970s, intellectuals and those responsible for the advocacy of cultural transformation have been calling attention to postmodern claims to truth and experience. Postmodernity is difficult to define, but quite simply represents much of what we have been discussing in this chapter: It is a challenge to the imperialistic privileges of modernity. The postmodern thinker reminds us that the kinds of truth or facticity maintained by modern science, rationalism, and empiricism are not the only valid aspects of modern knowledge and understanding. The postmodern mind protests the great white flood that bleaches everything in its path, making us think there is only one way, one truth. The postmodern thinker tells us to listen to the voices of those whom we sought to drown in the name of progress. Let those voices teach us; let them tell us what they know. There is no *one* meaning; there are many meanings. There is only what people tell us of their lives, their hopes, fears, and ways of ordering existence. Plurality is the corollary of postmodernity; yet behind postmodern thinking there is the religious assumption that there is *more than one meaning*. That notion is the wellspring of pluralism, for it moves beyond relativity to the possibility of the one in the many.

When we begin to comprehend what postmodern thinkers tell us, we realize that postmodernity has been a feature of the modern world almost from its beginnings. Women's struggle for a voice goes back at least to the early nineteenth century. "Listen to us; don't force your truth and your single-mindedness upon us," they said. Women even made postmodern claims as early as the seventeenth century, in the voices of Anne Hutchinson and Mary Dyer, perhaps also in the poetry of Anne Bradstreet. The spiritual adventures of Sarah Pierpont Edwards (wife of Jonathan) can be considered an episode in the emergence of postmodern protest. The right to speak, to act, to vote, to determine one's own thoughts without deference to the signification of white masculine modernism—these issues have evolved through the course of modern history into the present. Modernity and postmodernity exist side by side. They are not chronological phases but aspects of human experience that have acquired epic proportion since the nineteenth century and the advance of the technocorporate world as an entity unto itself, a principality and power that cannot be denied its sovereignty. But postmodernity claims that diversity is the desired shape of things.

Measuring the Plurality of Race and Gender

Race and gender are aspects of the struggle for the acceptance of diversity, a diversity that is no longer confined to institutions and established traditions. Religious ideas and practices spawned by race and gender are actively circulating among people who make no claims to religious institutional identity. They find their identity expressed in the community of those who share their protest; they find it expressed in the power of what they think and do. This diversity, of course, has adopted institutional forms. There are organizations that act as facilitators of ultimate order and meaning for the people who belong. Among African Americans there have been societies like the National Association for the Advancement of Colored People (NAACP), the Southern Christian Leadership Conference, the Student Nonviolent Coordinating Committee, and even the Urban League, all of which play a religious role in America alongside the many Baptist, Methodist, Holiness, and Pentecostal congregations and denominations. These organizations represent a worldview, a construction of reality.

The effect of gender upon diversity may be observed in the various feminist and womanist organizations, some of which are overtly religious in their fashioning of rituals, stories, and enclaves that signify the ultimate meaning of the feminine. There are covens of wicca that nurture the sense of original sacredness. The origins of life and of history are affirmed as female. The covens celebrate womanist assumptions and values as the original form of human religious behavior. In doing so, they provide ultimate signification for women. God is Goddess. The ultimate reality is female. "God" is a male concept and a male reality. "God" is remote and permits humans to devastate the earth to which they belong because He is concerned with His own expectations and lives only for the obedience of men in achieving domination over the earth. But the earth is The Holy, say these womanists. The earth is Gaia, not God. The earth is the holy mother who binds us together. She is the real divinity, the ultimate reality.

The Ethnic Posture

American history has been the story of the great Völkerwanderungen of humanity produced by the advent of the modern age. Large masses of people have been extracted from long-settled parts of the earth and transported into the coastlands, plains, meadows, and mountains of North America. In the nineteenth century these mass migrations involved great numbers of people, partly because of advances in shipbuilding technology. People came from Ireland, Germany, eastern Europe, Italy, and the eastern Mediterranean. They came as Jews and as Christians. But Jews from Russia and Poland were different, religiously and culturally, from Jews in Germany and North Africa. Catholic Christians from Poland were quite different, religiously and culturally, from Irish and French Catholics. And the Catholics of Italy and Sicily had their own distinctive religious cultures. Then, of course, there were those Christians from Greece,

Russia, Romania, and other parts of eastern Europe, Christians who thought of themselves as Catholics who had severed their ties with Rome and the Vatican in the eleventh century C.E. These were the Orthodox, who had lived for many centuries as members of ethnic cultures saturated with forms of Christianity unique to their own histories. These Orthodox churches were autocephalous (self-headed) national churches bound to each other in a doctrine maintained by bishops who were in communication across ethnic and national boundaries.

Religiousness, we remember, is not confined to the restrictions and definitions of "official" institutions. Jews are religious in ways other than what the rabbis condone or promote. People always have ideas and practices that are unique to their experiences or circumstances. The political, economic, and geographical elements of their lives require ceremonies, rituals, and stories that give meaning and shape to their existence. These ideas and practices may be supplemental to the official doctrines and rituals of their religion. They constitute forms of folk religion. They may be opposed, ignored, or approved by their official religious orders. Sometimes they become established ways of understanding or practicing the official doctrines and practices. Ethnicity itself is in many ways religious.

The Polish Catholic or the Romanian Orthodox person may have distinctively Polish or Romanian ways of celebrating the Resurrection of Jesus Christ. The Mass, the Divine Liturgy, and the Holy Eucharist may have specifically ethnic components and associations. Christians from different societies may have prayers and special rituals that are performed in families and villages, outside the churches, sometimes with the participation of priests, sometimes not. Similarly, the Jews of the Warsaw ghetto and the many shtetls of Poland and Russia developed practices and taught stories and ways of studying the Talmud that are distinctive of their cultural location.

When these Jewish peoples came to America in the nineteenth and twentieth centuries, they were displaced, religiously and culturally. Oftentimes thrown together in cities with people of other ethnic and national identities, they frequently sought separation. They were also taken aback by the already established Jewish communities of North America. Who were these people who called themselves Jews but who dressed like Protestant Americans, who built synagogues that looked like Presbyterian churches, and who didn't go to shul or study the Talmud? They were not real Jews, said the Jews of eastern Europe. They were Jews whitened by the flood of Americanism who called themselves Reform Jews. Ethnic assumptions and practices had produced great variety in American Judaism. Synagogues and communities were established to reconcile differences, but also to register disapproval. Many Jews wanted to have their Jewishness signified by the ways they had established during centuries of oppression and existence in alien societies. Ethnicity is a way of distinguishing a separate people; it is a group-conscious attempt to control identity and facilitate or resist change. To some extent ethnicity may be an artificial kind of signification; it exists only to the extent that a group identifies itself in a particular manner, for a particular reason. Some Poles may be almost indistinguishable from some Russians except by their insistence upon certain customs and their identification with a particular locale. When the locale is changed and the Poles suddenly find themselves within Russian borders, they will insist upon the differences and seek to survive as a distinct group with language and customs setting them apart as a construction of reality, a religious world of ultimate order and meaning.

In America, the diversity of social order has been significantly affected by this kind of ethnic religiousness. The Polish Catholic found it difficult to accept the language and practices of Hungarian Catholics. Germans for a time insisted upon the establishment of a German Catholic Church in America. The hierarchy resisted these ethnic demands and established an American Catholic Church based upon the geographical distinctions of parish and diocese that were inclusive of people from diverse backgrounds. However, ethnic religiousness continued to assert itself in the establishment of ethnic congregations. In many American cities it is possible to find a Hungarian Catholic church on one corner, across the street from a German Catholic church, with a Slovakian or Ukrainian church a block away and St. Bridget's a block farther on.

Ethnicity has demanded its own model in the course of the diversification of American religion. It has asserted itself in opposition to any notion of a melting of distinctions. The "melting pot" theory itself was a product of the flood of white Americanism that sought to shape the new republic according to the assumptions of modernism. To an extent, of course, the theory was successful. For a time all diversity was assimilated and accommodated in the commonality of the civil religion and the flexibility of the Protestantism that dominated the culture. It took the increasing diversity of the twentieth century, and a major challenge from African Americans, to transform the authority of white Americanism, of modernity, and allow the significations of race, gender, and ethnicity to assert their religious vitality and move American culture in the direction of pluralism.

Notes

1. Ben Winton, "New York, New Commitment," *Arizona Republic*, January 11, 1997, Religion section, p. D7.

2. Wade C. Roof and William McKinney, *American Mainline Religion* (New Brunswick, NJ: Rutgers University Press, 1992); and Robert C. Wuthnow, *The Restructuring of American Religion* (Princeton: Princeton University Press, 1988).

3. Ralph Ellison, quoted in Cornel West, *Race Matters* (Boston: Beacon Press, 1993), p. 1.

4. Hector St. John Crevecoeur, quoted in Giles Gunn, *New World Metaphysics* (New York: Oxford University Press, 1981), pp. 135–136.

5. See R. Laurence Moore, *Religious Outsiders and the Making of Americans* (New York: Oxford University Press, 1986), esp. chap. 7.

6. Eldridge Cleaver, *Soul on Ice* (New York: Dell Publishing Co., 1968).

7. James H. Cone, *Black Theology and Black Power* (New York: Seabury Press, 1969), p. 12.

8. See Reginald F. Hildebrand, *The Times Were Strange and Stirring* (Durham, NC: Duke University Press, 1995), esp. pts. 1, 2.

9. Horace Bushnell, *Christian Nurture* (New York: Charles Scribner, 1861), p. 237.

10. Henry H. Harbaugh, *The True Glory of Woman* (Philadelphia: Reformed Church Publication Board, 1858), p. xxii.

11. Harbaugh, p. xi.

12. Nancy Hardesty, *Your Daughters Shall Prophesy* (New York: Carlson Publishing, 1991).

13. Ibid., pp. 16–17.

14. Ibid., p. 39.

6

Secularity and Diversity

For people living in the last days of the twentieth century, the word "secular" has a different meaning from that conveyed in centuries before the nineteenth. The word is derived from the Latin *saeculum*, which refers to "this world," "this age." As Christianity sought to clarify its message, its faith and meaning, in the broad context of the Roman Empire and Graeco-Roman civilization, it thought of the Gospel as being "in this age" but not *of* it. There was the world, the age, as it developed, seemingly on its own terms; and there was the Kingdom of God, the age of God's new creation. The Church, as the Body of Christ, represented a realm "not of this age"; but it nevertheless spoke to this age, and its people lived in this age. As a matter of fact, the Gospel was a message, a dharma, *for* this age.

Secularity and the Secular

The word "secular," therefore, relates in some way to this age, this world. Its nuances of meaning are attached to the history of Christianity. Discerning the relationship between "this age, this world" and the Kingdom of God has been the cause of a plethora of ideas, institutions, and movements. When human beings try to determine how it can be possible to live in the two "worlds," they raise serious questions. Some start revolutions; some retreat into monasteries or separatist communities; some seek the reform of "this world" according to the principles of the "other world"; some pretend that "this world" is the only reality. Proponents of the latter belief exist in a negative state, determined by their opposition to an "other world." Yet if the "other world" does not exist and can make no claims, why should we define ourselves by its visions?

Nevertheless, in the modern era, the notion of "this world" came to have an empirical meaning. "This world" meant that which is available for experimentation and observation by the senses. Accordingly, "secular" referred to ordinary material reality, with no relation to affirmation about God or gods, no concern for faith, values, or matters of transcendence and intuition. In other words, the modern understanding of "secular" is satisfied with a world of observable data—the thingification of existence. "Secular," therefore, came to stand for the world unto itself (whatever that may mean).

It would seem rather obvious to any contemplative person that all understandings of "the world" are constructed, imagined. "We live in the description of a place and not in the place itself," wrote Wallace Stevens.[1] Actually, we live in the place we constantly imagine, describe, and construct. If we take this insight seriously, we would have to conclude that the idea of "this world unto itself" is itself an imaginative construct. "The secular" is just as much a manifestation of the religious aspect of humanity as are more traditionally sacred constructs.

The modern restrictive meaning of the word "secular" gave rise to secularization, a process in which a one-dimensional existence is affirmed. However, secularization means several things; there have been several manifestations (or stages) of this one-dimensional assumption.

The Process of Secularization in America

In its early stages secularization has referred to the gradual replacement of sacred institutions with institutions of a public, "this-worldly" origin. As William Clebsch has shown, "religion stirred successive aspirations of the American dream, aspirations which when transformed into achievements belonged no longer to the saints but to the citizenry."[2] Clebsch demonstrates how various campaigns for education, justice, the reform of society, and the care of the needy began with the advocacy and action of the churches. When the goals were either fulfilled or frustrated, secular institutions were then organized to carry on with the programs. This process by means of which issues of justice, welfare, health care, and education were removed from an ecclesiastical jurisdiction and given a new and independent organizational status is perhaps the first stage in what we mean by secularization.

Early in the twentieth century, when educators and early social scientists were commenting on the process of secularization, they tended to be satisfied with observing that pursuits like education had become more and more matters of public rather than ecclesiastical administration. Most intellectuals and academics seemed to be content with the liberation of public function from the control of the churches. To put the state or some privately endowed institution in charge of health care or education was to secularize that program. Hospitals, colleges, and schools became secular and public. Education and health were "this-worldly" enterprises that should be administered without the advice, consent, or design of the clergy and churches. As we can see from the vantage point of the late twentieth century, this was a very proscribed understanding of secularization. It did not, *could not*, accomplish its aim given the nature of American society at the time. That is because the sacred descriptions and practices of a people are never confined to the institutions that seek to regulate and enhance them.

Sacred matters and secular matters are always maintained in a dialectical tension; they become religious and cultural.

"Our Father's" World

American society was not "secularized" by virtue of the displacement of denominational jurisdictions. Society retained its own ideas about the ultimate order and meaning of existence; it was saturated with notions of a kindly Providence who directed the affairs of humankind and had made America the setting in which human dreams could be realized. The nation was still "under God"; Americans "believed" in God, in a morality perhaps more utilitarian than Christian (but nevertheless assumed to be "Christian"), and in an afterlife that justified a life of dedication, hard work, and "right" living. It was not only the persistence of such ideas that belied the claims of institutional secularization, but, as we observed in Chapter 4, there were sacred intentions and values behind many "secular" activities. Mother's Day, Father's Day, Flag Day, Armistice Day, even Labor Day and Arbor Day—all celebrated meaning that was not confined to "this age."

"This is my Father's world" is a Protestant hymn of the early twentieth century expressing the religious sense that lay behind all those "secular" events. It is worthy of analysis:

> This is my Father's world, And to my listening ears,
> All nature sings, And round me rings the music of the spheres,
> This is my Father's world: I rest me in the thought
> Of rocks and trees, of skies and seas; His hand the wonders wrought.
> This is my Father's world, The birds their carols raise,
> The morning light, the lily white, Declare their Maker's praise.
> This is my Father's world: He shines in all that's fair;
> In the rustling grass I hear Him pass, He speaks to me everywhere.
> This is my Father's world, O let me ne'er forget
> That though the wrong seems oft so strong, God is the ruler yet.
> This is my Father's world: The battle is not done;
> Jesus who died shall be satisfied, And earth and heaven be one.[3]

Nature, in all its aesthetic and scientific splendor, gives evidence of its creator—it is *all* His world. According to this very common perception, the ways of humanity, often so misdirected and seemingly autonomous, even anarchic, are indeed within the dominion of God. And the life of Jesus was not in vain; it was still in the process of achieving its goal of the unity of secular (this world, the "earth") and sacred ("heaven," obviously understood not to be confined to some after-death abode).

Although this hymn might be construed as belonging exclusively to those churches affected by the theological liberalism of the late nineteenth and early twentieth centuries, that theological liberalism was itself a response to the claims of those who suggested that the world was secular because it was no longer subject to ecclesiastical governance.[4] Many educators, particularly the presidents of public universities, were quick to acknowledge that theirs was a religious, even a "Christian" mission. They were charged with preparing the nation's youth for responsible and dedicated participation in a society where values were important.

American culture was by no means secular. The process of secularization had merely shifted to a different level. The term "Judeo-Christian" came into use so that Jews and Christians might share a supposed "common ground" at the foundation of American society. Many Jews and Christians were willing to sacrifice much of the particularity of their traditions, suppressing their distinctive identities. In the face of the increased diversity of American society, Jews and Christians could presumably make common cause, accepting their differences in deference to a greater good that might be served in a more pluralistic "Our Father's world." We have the same Father, they agreed. For many Christians, Christianity was belief in God, and the teaching of Jesus was (presumably) about "the fatherhood of God and the brotherhood of man" and a sense of immortality. Many Jews could affirm the same notions, accepting even Jesus as a good, moral teacher, even if he was superseded by Moses and the prophets in their advocacy of the same principles.

There is considerable evidence to suggest that the world was still not "on its own," even after the disengagement of ecclesiastical institutions from much of public life. All during this time there remained an "established" religious order that underlay the structure of society and culture.

The Post-Christian Era

The third stage in the development of the secularity of "this worldliness" is evidenced in the "death-of-God theology" and the "post-Christian era" rhetoric of the 1960s. It is interesting that this final declaration of "this world's" independence of Christianity occurred at the same time that a new religiousness began to manifest itself in the "protesting" culture of the 1960s. Like the Reformation programs of Martin Luther, John Calvin, and the sixteenth-century radical reformers, the so-called American "cultural revolution" of the 1960s was a *pro*test on behalf of a "new order" and a protest *against* the established order of several centuries of traditional worldviews, morality, and experience. The 1960s were a time of religious revolution, a historical moment in which the victory of modernity over traditional and established religion was, at least rhetorically, completed. It was the final stage in the development of the modern secular mind that sought to make the meaning and order of existence a matter of calculation, efficiency, and existential decision. The earlier stages of modern secularization were finally recognized for what they were—a partial wresting of the control of human destiny from ecclesiastical direction, without losing commonly acceptable notions of transcendent value.

During the early 1950s and the Eisenhower era, America had been the scene of what many referred to as a "religious revival." What was meant was a revival of interest in something called "religion." It was the climactic season of common-cause religion, which required little precision of thought. "Religion" is a good thing, was the assumption. Even "God" could be a common reference that enabled the Gallup Poll to determine the extremely high percentage of Americans who "believed in God." The pledge of allegiance to the American flag incorporated the phrase *"one nation, under God,* indivisible, with liberty and justice for all." Some Christian and Jewish theologians rejected this "religion-in-general" notion and objected to the use of God's name without substantive doctrinal reference. There were those who said that Christianity itself had become so close to American culture that it had been absorbed by, and identified with, that culture. Christianity had, in other words, become "culture religion."

Peter Berger, who was to become one of America's most eminent sociologists while at the same time maintaining a very sophisticated theological vocation, authored *The Noise of Our Solemn Assemblies,* a reference to the meaningless participation in American church life that ignored the God of Israel and of Christ who waited patiently outside those "solemn assemblies" to call people of faith to risk their lives on behalf of truth and justice.[5] Historian Martin Marty struggled to find *The New Shape of American Religion.*[6] Perhaps Christian faith can be freed from its cultural bondage (what sociologist Gibson Winter called *The Suburban Captivity of the Churches)*[7] and recover its integrity. Perhaps the churches can become the advocates of God's Kingdom in the Kingdom of "this world" (the *saeculum).* The end of the 1950s and the beginning of the 1960s was one of the most exciting periods of American intellectual and cultural history. There were profound challenges to the status quo in human rights, education, religion, art, music, and morality.

Thinkers like Berger, Marty, Winter, and Will Herberg were probably accurate in their assessments of American religion. The media took note and gave their ideas considerable public exposure. None was more preeminent than the elder statesman of postmodern American religious thought, Reinhold Niebuhr, one of the most significant thinkers of the mid-twentieth century. Niebuhr, over the course of several decades, challenged the prevailing understanding of American religion and culture in book after book and in essays in distinguished journals like the *Atlantic,* the *New Republic, The Nation,* and *The Christian Century.* The criticism of the times was directed at religion, politics, economics, and other aspects of American culture.

This wealth of social and religious criticism was significant for many reasons, but notably it served to facilitate the spread of modern secularization. Critics both inside and outside the continuing religious order began to refer to the "end of the Protestant era" and then to the end of the Christian era. The "post-Christian era" was proclaimed. The dominant Protestant influence over the evolution of American culture and religious life had been eroding for some time, and it became obvious with the birth of the "Judeo-Christian" rhetoric that the end was nigh for the Protestant hegemony. Nevertheless, it was traumatic for many to be told that they were living in a "post-Christian" world. In the minds of an American public, nurtured for so long on churchgoing (or on its counterpart, "synagogue going"), God-talk, and what critic Harold Bloom[8] refers to as America's love affair with Jesus, the end of the Christian era was beyond comprehension. What would America be without those signposts, those points of reference? God might get fed up with "the noise of our solemn assemblies," but at least there was a God to judge, to get "fed up"; at least those solemn assemblies were places where His name was respected, where He could be heard and spoken to.

The extent to which the "post-Christian era" has really emerged is difficult to evaluate. Perhaps this is simply a new stage in the history of Christianity itself. Nevertheless, rhetoric has its own way of creating worlds, and from the perspective of the last days of this twentieth century, perhaps the rhetoric signifies the end of the modern secularization process. "This world" stands by itself, in its functioning and in the language it uses to get on with the business of living. There can be no real significance to "the Kingdom of God" for the intellectuals and technicians of "this age" (the secular world) unless, of course, the corporate world were to perceive some advantage to "religiousness" for the self-esteem and efficiency of its workers.

The Sacredness of the Secular

"This is the age of the secular city," wrote Harvey Cox in his popular book *The Secular City.*

> Through supersonic travel and instantaneous communications its ethos is spreading into every corner of the globe. The world looks less and less to religious rules and rituals for its morality or its meanings. For some, religion provides a hobby, for others a mark of national or ethnic identification, for still others an aesthetic delight. For fewer and fewer does it provide an inclusive and commanding system of personal and cosmic values and explorations.[9]

The academic discipline of religious studies was at this time in the process of being born, its conception partly the result of the liberation of culture from Christian dominance. In his book, Cox avoided the religious studies question of whether the "rules and rituals" of the secular city were themselves subject to religious analysis and whether they might have been indicative of a new religious order. For Cox, God himself stood behind the secular city, pushing humanity to a new stage of faith and freedom.

Time magazine published a cover, black in mourning, edged in red, its white letters raising the ominous question: Is God Dead? In 1966, the year of *The Secular City*'s second printing, William Hamilton, a theologian on the faculty of Colgate Divinity School, noted that the theologian is "a man without faith, without hope, with only the present, with only love to guide him." His words echoed the sentiment of a variety of thinkers who announced the death of God and gave both a somber and celebratory tone to the secular victory. "Faith in God in the classical Christian tradition has always meant this," said Hamilton; "an act of passionate, personal daring and courage can be made, and when it is made, a real other is made known, over against man, making demands and making Himself known. This is the meaning of faith in God. It is this God of faith, made known in this way . . . who is no more."[10] By attending to this death of God and getting on with doing what we have to do, with no concern for any *meaning* to it all, the secular age has been fashioned.

Thirty years after Hamilton's intonation we are sobered by the fact that the diversity of American religion has been *extended* by the secular model. Once "this world" turned its back on the old "Christian" and "Judeo-Christian" orders, the gates of culture were opened. "Religions" are alive and well in an age that tries to manage its social, political, and cultural life as if religion did not exist. We might even say that secularity itself is a new religion of power, but that the proliferation of religions in the secular age is both a challenge to and a product of that secular religious power. We can certainly see this in many parts of the world where secular authority is opposed by religious ethnicity and by religions that affirm the separate identity of a people in the face of the totalitarian homogenization of the secular establishment. The presence of Muslims, Catholics, Africans, Native Americans, and Buddhists protests the religious assumptions of the secular establishment. "Give us whatever feeds and clothes our people," they say, "but do not try to force your curious values upon us and try to destroy our communities and our customs."

A New Religious Landscape

It may not be coincidental that the religious revolution of the 1960s, the advent of the secular city, and the "death of God" were accompanied by a new immigration act in 1965. The act, initiated by President Kennedy, ruled that immigration could no longer be regulated by exclusion based upon race, nationality, or religion. The way was open for the immigration of Asians, whose participation in the creation of the American republic had been stifled by such laws as the Chinese Exclusion Act of 1880. One hundred years after the passage of that law, the sacred landscape of America was changing radically.

The American landscape had been given its shape by the spires of New England meetinghouses and by the red brick cupolas and bell towers of Methodist, Baptist, and Presbyterian church buildings. In the east, in places like Pennsylvania, the early Lutheran and Reformed churches had adjacent cemeteries, their gray monuments rising and falling against the green hillsides. And the urban churches imposed their sandstone and limestone structures topped with crosses onto the skylines. Since the 1980s, primarily as a result of the new immigration act and the effects of wars and corporate invasions, the landscape has changed radically. There are Buddhist, Jain, Hindu, and Sikh temples and monasteries across America. Mosques and their minarets alter the sense of order in many cities and towns where Arabs, Africans, and Southeast Asians now reside. In the America of the 1990s, the sacred is manifested in communities of people from every part of the earth. In a land of such great diversity, sacred buildings are important because the towns and villages by themselves are no longer representative of a sacred world in which a special people lives, with its ceremonies and its celebratory lore. Religious communities must now rely on buildings to preserve their sacred ways and provide identity in the midst of a world that shows little sign of their influence. Asian peoples, whose temples have often been places for private prayers and offerings and centers for seasonal festivals, now must fashion houses for *gatherings*—partly because American religious life has always favored gatherings, assemblies, and associations.

The American landscape reveals the monuments of its religious diversity; these buildings are necessary because people must sort themselves out from the rest of their neighbors in order to maintain their sacred identities in a world that has been homogenized by shopping malls, television, computers, and credit cards. The presence of Asian and Middle Eastern peoples has radically diversified a landscape that no longer honors traditional ways, and has even transformed the sacred customs of its Christian forebears into secular festivals of consumerism. Christmas and Easter exist not as celebrations of the Nativity and Resurrection of Jesus Christ, but as occasions for gift giving and sentimental incantations about peace, good will, and the coming of spring and fertility. In this context the distinctiveness of Christianity is difficult to preserve because many of its traditional ideas and practices have been transformed into "holiday" activities and "Hallmark" sentiments that express the values of the consumer culture. In a sense, Christianity is denied its contribution to diversity on behalf of an imposed cultural order. The result is not a genuine pluralism because Christianity itself is not accepted as part of the diversity. It is accepted only to the extent that it remains a private, subjective affair. Its public role has been usurped by the technocorporate social order.

Many Americans will remember the television series *Kung Fu*, which was cast in the early 1970s. The series was symbolic of the post-Christian era and the advent of radical diversity. Its central character was an Asian who had been initiated as a lad into the mysterious ways of meditation, mindfulness, and sensory emancipation. Americans watched this young man use his powers of concentration and physical liberation to bring justice to the settlements of the American West. Most of those who watched the series did not realize that they were being drawn to a worldview that is very different from the religious orientations of traditional Judaism and Christianity. If they were aware of the "alien" religious presence, they did not care. However, this is partly because the new religious perspective was still being cast in a plot that was acceptable to Americans. The series was set in the familiar western American world where justice was swift and where the bad guys were always made to pay for their cruelty and unjust behavior. "Western" movies and novels have always held a fascination for Americans because they have traditionally maintained simple distinctions between right and wrong, good and evil, and have assured audiences and readers that evil would be punished and good rewarded.

But *Kung Fu* would not likely have been a popular American entertainment prior to 1965 and the new immigration act. It would not have been an acceptable aspect of popular culture prior to that stage in the secularization process when the cultural dominance of the Christian era was dislodged. Even in its own time the series was still transitional, despite the fact that it was cast in the familiar setting of the Western. It was not until the 1980s that the significance of the new diversity was made evident in the altered sacralization of the landscape itself.

Differentiation and Diversity

Sociologists, in their analyses of modernity, have called attention to differentiation, conventionalization, and demystification as characteristics of modern society and culture. Secularity accepts these characteristics as positive. No doubt they have enabled the creation of many technological marvels. Americans were not as aware of their significance, of course, until they were ready to announce the post-Christian era and the death of God. However, these three characteristics contribute to religious diversity and set forth a mandate for pluralism that the modern secular world has not been able to affirm.

Differentiation refers to the fragmentation of a previously and essentially "coinherent" world, which is dispersed into numerous components of knowledge and activity. If we may assume that the modern world gradually dissipates traditional societies, then we may observe the roughly five-hundred-year span of modernity during which various forms of human thought and action became separated from each other to the point where they often engaged in mutual conflict. A clear case in point is the presumed "conflict" between science and religion. If science refers to the pursuit and content of knowledge ("knowing," *scientia*), and if religion refers to the manner in which being is affirmed as ultimately ordered and meaningful, then there can be no "conflict." To know anything is to assume that whatever is observed, investigated, and described is also dependable—we may have confidence in our assumptions. There is no "conflict" in a traditional society because there is no "science," no "religion." There are only the multitude of ideas and activities that are integrated as a total mode of existence. There is little differentiation in these facets of existence; they exist interdependently. Whatever differentiation exists is determined primarily by time and space, by seasons and places, and by knowing what to do and how to do it in season and in place. Everything "coinheres." Even if it were possible to translate concepts effectively, it would be pointless to visit a traditional society and inquire about their "science" and their "religion." If we were finally to convince them of the importance and meaning of our inquiry, we would also be exiling them from their world into the "modern" world. We would be engaging in an act of colonialism, which takes away the voice of the people of the traditional world and makes them the victims of our modern significations.

In 1957, H. Richard Niebuhr delivered the Montgomery Lectures on Contemporary Civilization at the University of Nebraska. They served as the heart of a later book entitled *Radical Monotheism and Western Culture*. Niebuhr's radical monotheism is not so much an "ism" as it is a point of view, a kind of *via negativa*, a way of getting to the truth by denying absolute value to any partial claims to the truth. One might say that it is a way of denying *any claim* to the truth, inasmuch as the One is always greater than any of its parts, or even the sum total thereof. Niebuhr wants us to understand this "radical faith" as distinguishing the Hebraic and Christian ways from the coinherent ways of traditional societies.

"The emergence of radical monotheism in the West," writes Niebuhr, "took place ... at a time prior to the now conventional separation of our cultural activities into such domains as the religious, the political, the scientific, the economic, and the aesthetic."[11] Moses, for example, was the founder of a people, a social order. He was a leader, a lawgiver, even somewhat of a poet. Our modern conventions of differentiation seek to conventionalize him solely as a religious or ethical figure. Similarly, we place Israel's great "prophets" into a category of exclusively religious differentiation that does not observe their eccentric and "antireligious" characters as poets, reformers, political radicals, and "originators of a new literary style."

Niebuhr's "radical monotheism" is a virtually nontheistic posture that denies absolute status to any religion, cultural phenomenon such as "science," or concept. Radical monotheism makes possible a commitment to the whole of being, thereby permitting acceptance of pluralism on behalf of a good beyond all partial claims, yet recognizing the participation of diverse ideas and traditions *in* the whole of being or the greater good.

The differentiation and conventionalization that are aspects of secularization contribute to greater diversity while at the same time precluding any attempt to understand human religiousness in relation to the greater good, trying to limit it to the conventional category of "religion." Therefore, secularity and science, for example, are excluded from religious criticism and religion is denied its role in the furtherance of pluralism.

Secularization leads to differentiation because when we make "this world" autonomous we are forced to deny any holistic significance to ideas and practices that acknowledge another dimension to reality. "This world" becomes something we must imagine, analyze, manipulate, and fashion according to our own human judgments. Therefore we must "chop it up" or "break it down" into workable components. We make these judgments according to what we perceive to be the kinds of questions we must deal with and the usefulness we must organize. We establish classifications and conventions. One particular aspect of existence can be separated from others and called the "economic" aspect because it deals with laws that concern the availability of the necessities of human existence—matters of sustenance (food, clothing, shelter, communication, transportation, and so on). Economics therefore becomes a distinctive convention, differentiated from other conventions even though it cannot really extricate itself from questions of ultimate order and meaning. In a manner of speaking, there is no such thing as "economics"; it is an invention, a signification of modernity.

Many other conventions emerge, differentiated from each other and requiring humans and their activities to be classified as political, religious, scientific, or aesthetic. But from this point of view *all* of *these* conventions except the religious are thought to be "secular"—of this age, this world. Religion then becomes the conventionalization of the larger questions of being, order, and meaning in such a way that it is charged with being "otherworldly," irrelevant, or private.

The differentiation resulting from secularization opens the doors of human creativity to great religious diversity. If religion is a private and optional matter, then human religiousness will become anxious and creative in the search for a story and a "path" that will enable people to know that they are part of an ordered and meaningful cosmos. This anxiety and creativity may remain somewhat privatized, so that we may almost facetiously imagine a diversification that is as extensive as the population. All people think that they have constructed an entirely private religious life—the fruits of "Me-ism." This assumption is quite illusory, of course. All ideas and actions are to some degree derivative and relational.

Differentiation shapes religious diversity not only in the caricature of "Me-ism," but also in the plethora of so-called "new religions." Japan and the United States have been the scenes of a great increase in the rise of "new religions" since the 1960s. Secularization has released the religious impulse so that many sects and cults have emerged to fill the void created by the apparent dysfunctional character of established traditions. Secularization releases the hold of established traditions upon society and culture. Nevertheless, these traditions—like Buddhism, Christianity, and Judaism—have great and diverse histories that are richer in experience, ideas, and practice than either the "members" of the traditions or the general public is aware of. There are many Buddhisms because there are many Buddhists. And there may be elements of Buddhism that were expressed in a certain time and place that are suddenly rediscovered by people who are searching for a vision of reality that deconstructs the aimlessness and fragmentation of contemporary existence. New religions tend to be eclectic. Their charismatic leaders have the religious resources of an entire world, past and present, available to them. They find resources in the wealth of a great diversity of traditions; and, in the freedom and entrepreneurialism created by secularization, they fashion a great many new religions that attract millions of people.

The Religious Diversity of Secularity

Religious diversity is compounded by the secularists themselves. It is difficult to affirm the self-sufficiency of "this age," "this world," without trying to *imagine* what that means. Secularists tend to divide themselves into a variety of "this-worldly" religious groups. There are the accommodationists, those whose lives are largely unexamined, but who imagine that the meaning of life is limited to what the corporate, commercial, and consumerist world portrays. They accommodate to *what is*, say "no" to very little, and can imagine no other perception of reality. There are also the nihilists, who conscientiously maintain that there is no meaning or significance to existence; therefore people should do what they have to do with little regard for others or for the future. The deterministic secularists are those who regard everything as materially and scientifically interconnected. There are no "accidents," they affirm; but people can alert themselves to the circumstances in which they exist in order to prepare themselves for what is bound to happen, and accept the inevitable results without gratitude or disappointment. Naturalists are usually aesthetic determinists. They observe everything as an ingredient in the course of nature, but reserve for themselves a certain appreciative awareness of nature and walk in the beauty of its passage. Perhaps the aesthetic character of their naturalism qualifies their determinism, insofar as appreciative awareness may set us outside the ongoing course of nature. But naturalism is nature-ism, an ideology or system of ideas and behavior derived from a this-worldly, materialist view of all reality. The humanist is a naturalist who makes a great deal out of the human transcendence of nature, giving humanity a degree of responsibility for the valuation and fulfillment of nature's potential. Humans are *in* nature, but not entirely *of* it. However, humanism is a form of secular "this-world-ism" that permits no transcendence beyond the material observations of technical, empirical reason.

Demystification as Diversity

Secularization demystifies the world. When secularists use the word "mystery," they are usually referring to a problem that is *not yet solved* and therefore remains a "mystery." Mystery, for the secularist, is an element in the process of understanding the material, knowable order of things. The mystery novel takes its thematic assumptions from the modern, secularist notion of mystery. In this form of fiction, all knowledge is a matter of assembling *all* of the facts of a given situation and then applying technical reason toward discovering the solution. The secularist always assumes that the circumstances of life can be defined as problems that require skills to solve. For example, environmental concerns pose "problems" that must be solved. If there is pollution, then an appointment of engineers, attorneys, and business people must be arranged. These experts are charged with defining the "problem" and determining a "solution": What is causing the pollution? How shall we correct the situation?

It would be absurd to say that we should not cease our pollution-generating activities or that we should not screen out the pollutants. But the environmental crisis is not a problem; it is a religious concern, a question of our perception of reality. If there is no creative transformation of our perception of reality, there will be no end to the crisis. The problem-solving mentality, left to itself, will simply create more "problems" to solve.

The mystery novel assumes the definition of a problem and a solution of "mystery." We discover, finally, that the estranged wife or butler "did it"; the mystery is "solved." However, we may discover that the whole of being is a mystery of which we are parts. Mystery is not "solved"; instead, mystery is what we *encounter in* everything we know or experience.

When we say that we "know" something, it means that we are trying to describe the indescribable, define the undefinable. Theories, like Einstein's conception of relativity, are genuinely imaginations of mystery. *What we know* is very much mystery. But the modern secularized culture tends to think of mystery as what we do *not yet* know and will one day "solve," thus putting an end to the "mystery."

Secularization has engaged in a serious campaign of demystification that seeks to bring everything under the illusion of human manipulation and control. For centuries human beings have been fascinated by the moon. The Japanese poet Bashō filled his consciousness with the presence of the moon.

The crescent moon—
The eastern sky is dark,
And the sound of a bell.
On the autumn lake, faintly
Someone playing an old tune on the
koto.[12]

Today we look at the moon and know that it holds no magic. We have been there! Our technology has "conquered" the moon. And what we have learned to control or master, we assume no longer has mystery. "How wonderful it is in this land of ours," wrote Bashō on his visit to Shiogama, "that even in remote and unfrequented places such as this, the divine power of the gods is omnipotent." To the secular mind, this is sheer naïveté, or at best poetic license.

Many theologians and sociologists of religion have pointed out that this demystification of the world began with the advent of Hebraic and Christian worldviews represented in the Bible. Yahweh (God) was thought to be separate from the nature he created; and humankind (the *image* of God) was separate from the "rest" of nature. Although this may be somewhat true, it is an oversimplification. Peter Berger, in *The Sacred Canopy,* makes the case for the "Biblical" demystification of the world, as does Harvey Cox in *The Secular City.* Cox looked upon demystification as the divinely mandated liberation of the world, enabling humanity to get on with the task of making existence "more human." But Berger is not as sanguine as Cox about this demystification; he remains convinced that the world left to itself ignores the sacred and has no foundation for its values or its integrity.

However, the demystification represented in Judaism and Christianity is actually a sacralization of *all of being,* as Richard Niebuhr has shown. Sacredness is a *shared* reality; therefore no one element in the order of creation can claim ultimate sacrality. The story of the Bible is the story of *shared* sacredness: God creates in order to express "relationship." He makes covenant with humanity, first by telling Abraham to "depart" from his country, his place of nativity, his father's house. "Take a risk" is the message; "See that other lands and places are sacred, too. You will never be able to keep your sacred world as if it were yours alone. The whole of Being is sacred because it lives by covenant, by relationship." James Weldon Johnson's "The Creation" made this point:

> *And God stepped out on space,*
> *And he looked around and said:*
> *I'm lonely—*
> *I'll make me a world.*

And so the story began. Johnson provides a beautiful portrait of the unfolding of it all. Everything fit. Everything related.

> *Then God walked around,*
> *And God looked around*
> *On all that he had made.*
> *He looked at his sun,*
> *And he looked at his moon,*
> *And he looked at his little stars;*
> *He looked on his world*
> *With all its living things,*
> *And God said, I'm lonely still.*

And so God thought about it all. And then,

> *This Great God,*
> *Like a mammy bending over her baby,*
> *Kneeled down in the dust*
> *Toiling over a lump of clay*
> *Till he shaped it in his own image.*[13]

The idea of "Creation" is not the separation of Being, so that only God is sacred. It is the sharing of Being, of covenant, so that all things exist only in relationship. Relationship is mystery. Relationship cannot be defined, only lived.

The secular mind abhors mystery. But so does the kind of religious mind that seeks to make everything a matter of "simple faith," the religious mind that is concerned primarily with its private salvation, something it can claim as inner sacredness. This type of religious mind abhors mystery—it wants no priests, no temples, no sacrifices, no sacred groves, no festival days, no special people who have been born in a place where the Great God kneeled down in the dust like a mammy kneeling over her baby. This kind of religious mind is very modern; it makes common cause with the secular mind and produces a demystified world. Perhaps that is good; perhaps that is as it should be. Perhaps the liberation has been good. Except for the fact that many human beings have been unable to live with this liberation. For them it seems as though their freedom has been trampled in the rhetoric of liberation. Someone "in authority" has said that it is impossible, unnecessary, and unintelligent to indulge in "mystery"—the truth is in possession of those in power who deny that there is any other permissible or creditable way. Indigenous peoples, whose religiosity is comprehensive and filled with mystery that is conveyed and symbolized by activities that the secular perspective considers to be magical, superstitious, illusory, or mystifying, are denied a legitimate voice in intellectual and cultural dialogue. They are "primitive," benighted, ignorant, or anachronistic, waiting to be elevated to a more enlightened mode of perception. But suddenly the mysteried ways of the indigenous peoples spring to life. They begin to crowd the graveyards where skeletons of mystery do a danse macabre. The great diversity of religions, living, dead, and resurgent, springs to life with the addition of the "primitive" ways we had left behind in our rationalistic smugness.

Demystification breeds reaction, perhaps because mystery cannot be denied. And so people turn to the new religions, or probe the old ones, for some satisfaction. Religious resurgence abounds. One of the results of the search for mystery will be uncritical involvement in movements that may call for more knowledgeable judgment; another will be the mystification of those areas of popular culture where musical groups and counterculturists dabble in strange rites and incantations. And so the diversity increases.

Notes

1. Wallace Stevens, quoted in Martin E. Marty, *A Nation of Behavers* (Chicago: University of Chicago Press, 1976), pp. 3, 184.

2. William A. Clebsch, *From Sacred to Profane America* (New York: Harper & Row, 1968), p. 2.

3. This 1901 hymn is by Maltbie D. Babcock. In Armin Haeussler, *The Story of Our Hymns* (St. Louis: Eden Publishing House, 1952), pp. 116–117.

4. For an interpretation of theological and religious liberalism, see my *Religion in the New World: The Shaping of Religious Traditions in the United States* (Minneapolis: Fortress Press, 1990), chap. 17; see also Kenneth Cauthen, *The Impact of American Religious Liberalism* (New York: Harper & Brothers, 1962).

5. Peter Berger, *The Noise of Our Solemn Assemblies* (Garden City, NY: Doubleday, 1961).

6. Martin E. Marty, *The New Shape of American Religion* (New York: Harper & Row, 1958).

7. Gibson Winter, *The Suburban Captivity of the Churches* (Garden City, NY: Doubleday, 1961).

8. Harold Bloom, *The American Religion* (New York: Simon & Schuster, 1992), cf. pp. 32, 40, 65.

9. Harvey Cox, *The Secular City* (New York: Macmillan, 1966).

10. William Hamilton, quoted in Edwin S. Gaustad, *A Documentary History of Religion in America*, vol. 2 (Grand Rapids, MI: Wm. B. Eerdmans, 1982), p. 519.

11. H. Richard Niebuhr, *Radical Monotheism and Western Culture* (New York: Harper & Row).

12. Makoto Ueda, *Matsuo Bashō* (Tokyo: Kodansha International, 1982), p. 83.

13. James Weldon Johnson, *God's Trombones* (New York: Penguin, 1981), pp. 17–20.

7

The New Age as
a Festival of Diversity

Americans have always been possessed by the dream, the religious sense that there was an original paradise, a harmony that will be restored in a new age. As William Clebsch demonstrated in his *American Religious Thought,* there is a constant theme at work in America—the idea of "being at home in the universe."[1] Whether we examine the thought of Jonathan Edwards, Ralph Waldo Emerson, or William James, we discover a consciousness of the integral beauty of nature, society, and deity. There is the conviction that those with eyes to see will discover in nature an original paradise not ordinarily observed. Even feminist thinkers like Mary Daly and Carol Christ believed that a "gynocentric," egalitarian, peaceful, and ecologically harmonious world existed prior to the rise of patriarchy. What becomes somewhat apparent, though still hidden, in their thinking is that the globalization and diversification of religion in contemporary America have provided the context in which colonialism, patriarchy, and rationalism can be overcome and paradise restored.

The religious diversity of our time has provided an occasion of feasting called the New Age. The religious quest for paradise, a new age, a return to Eden has gathered into its imagination the wisdom of Asia, Native America, and the holiness of the American landscape. In this perspective, diversity is the sign of the New Age dawning; the whole of history has been groaning in travail until now.

"A leaderless but powerful network is working to bring about radical change *in the United States,*" wrote Marilyn Ferguson in *The Aquarian Conspiracy* (italics mine). Her "conspiracy" was a serendipitous coming together of forces that represented the beginning of "a millennium of love and light—in the words of the popular song, 'The Age of Aquarius,' the time of 'the mind's true liberation.'"[2] A new mind was being fashioned, said Ferguson, an "intimate joining," quite unexpected—except, of course, by those who were convinced it had arrived. In Ferguson's thought, there was no time to try to fix things up in this curiously deranged world. A "new mind" was being shaped that was triggering a radical change in thought and action. Scientists, philosophers, physicians, and politicians were among the conspirators whose minds were uniting for the sake of the earth.

The Ascendant Conspiracy

"The great shuddering, irrevocable shift overtaking us is not a new political, religious, or philosophical system," said Ferguson. It was instead, she maintained, "the ascendance of a startling worldview"—which in any reasonable exercise of religious criticism is exactly what religion represents. Religion always has to do with new birth, new perception, the resurrection of a new body, not like the old. This new birth, new perception—this ascending worldview of which Ferguson writes—gathers together the discoveries of theoretical science and insights from earliest recorded thought, this itself an insight of the New Thought movement of Helena Blavatsky and others in the nineteenth century.

The uniqueness of the conspiracy, according to Ferguson, was that no great statistical measure was available. The conspirators did not associate in clubs, parties, ideological group, or lodges. "You find instead little clusters and loose networks." Sooner or later these people connected; their numbers grew. We may note here a mysteried attachment to the conspiracy and its great transformation.

The "little clusters and loose networks" are like the Pietist conventicles of the eighteenth-century Lutheran and Reformed traditions, the Methodist classes of the Church of England, and the Hasidic courts of eastern European Judaism. They usually purport to be the renewal and perpetuation of a lost or disregarded way of life—whether that be true Christianity, true Judaism, or the true path of divine immanence. Pietism in Christianity and Hasidism in Judaism were both movements for a *people's* appropriation of religious experience, appropriations that would renew their traditions.

Ferguson's "Aquarian Conspiracy" depends upon the advances in knowledge and human potential that can account for a new age in which human consciousness takes into itself the divine immanence essential to a harmonious universe. However, she is also aware of the fact that this consciousness and harmony have been around for a long time, and that now they can come of age—the world and the ancient tradition renewed and fulfilled. Over the centuries, she tells us, techniques and instruments of mind liberation and transformation have been known. There have been paradigmatic persons and experiences; there have been initiates into the soul of what becomes the Age of Aquarius. Ferguson writes:

> Scattered brotherhoods, religious orders and small groups explored what seemed to be extraordinary reaches of conscious experience. In their esoteric

doctrines, they sometimes wrote of the liberating quality of their insights. But they were too few, they had no way to disseminate their discoveries widely, and most of earth's inhabitants were preoccupied with survival, not transcendence. Quite suddenly in *this* decade [the 1970s], these deceptively simple systems and their literature, the riches of many cultures, are available to whole populations.[3]

There is little doubt that the notion of ascendant conspiracy (itself a religious concept) had been given a tremendous fusion of rhetorical power by the cultural revolution of the 1960s. The immigration law of 1965 certainly had much to do with making available "to whole populations" all those techniques, doctrines, and recorded experiences that were necessary to the faith in conspiracy. The old cultural establishment had been shaken to its foundations and the "post-Christian era" ushered in. What was to take the place of the Kingdom of God, a symbol important to both Judaism and Christianity, and one that had been basic to America's cultural understanding?[4] What did all these "new" techniques and the talk of raised consciousness mean? Did they belong together in some way? What were we to do with the diversity of transformational themes and systems?

The Vision Born

By the early 1980s, the religious power of conspiracy had gathered enough momentum to permit a holistic vision of the many systems and experiences. There was a Church of the Earth Nation and a new periodical entitled *Earth Nation Sunrise*. It was time to shun the old competitive religiousness, time to turn one's back on the exclusivist religious claims of many emissary traditions like Christianity, Islam, and Buddhism. Face the new, not the old; face the dawn of the Earth Nation.

Finally, as *Earth Nation Sunrise* announced, human beings had begun to recognize the peaceful, harmonious coexistence of other sentient creatures who lived on the planet. Finally, there existed communities of human beings who had learned from the other creatures the importance of unity and harmony. These communities were linked by their discovery of a "new mind." They were coalescing "national non-organizations" (Ferguson's term) "for a *new age on earth* which shall be the embodiment of every positive thought we hold in our minds, just as the old age embodied our fears. The construction has begun of a new reality, where the mysteries are revealed within each human being as s/he comes into harmony with the planet as a whole. We celebrate this sunrise."[5] The idea of the New Age had taken hold. Although many of its roots are in New Thought[6] and its assumptions in harmony with Pietism, the New Age movement relies significantly on the insights and concerns of twentieth-century scientific theory, the anxiety over ecological destruction, and the deluge of religious ideas and practices that have been part of the radical pluralism of America since the 1960s.

Mary Farrell Bednarowsky, commenting on the theological imagination of the New Age movement, relies somewhat on David Spangler's designation of the movement as a constellation of groups, "intentional spiritual communities" that represent the emerging consciousness of an Earth Nation. Bednarowsky claims that any attempt to understand the theology of the New Age movement must examine the work of these "intentional communities."[7] She insists that the more popular and diffuse aspects of New Age culture do not yield themselves to effective theological analysis. This limitation seems to stem from the American tendency to insist upon "association" as the key to understanding religion. However, we know that voluntary associations are not the only manifestations of the social expression of religiousness. The "tribe," "the people," the "Body of Christ," all represent an aspect of religious modality that is less contractual and associational than the notion of intentional communities. And certainly one of the important characteristics of the New Age movement is its dispersive and pervasive form. It does not lend itself to definition, at least in this moment of history. Although small groups and conventicles may be characteristic of the New Age, so are the factors of "non-organization," new consciousness, media invention, mind cure, universalism, divine immanentism, and a life-death continuity that permits communication between the two "realms" (implying the immutability of energy or life force, and the deathlessness of conscious energy).

Theological analysis of New Age religiousness cannot ignore the above-mentioned factors and characteristics. Religious criticism also must consider these factors, insofar as it constitutes the analysis and evaluation of the ways in which people strive to discern ultimate order and meaning in the course of existence. If, indeed, the New Age emerges out of the diversity and secularity of the late twentieth century, it must of necessity represent a form of religiousness related to *this moment* of history, one that is to be distinguished from the order imposed upon religious, social, and cultural life by modernistic rationality, "contractualism," and the individualism of the eighteenth and nineteenth centuries. Religious life in this moment tends to be explosive, rebellious, adventuresome, and somewhat anarchic. Intentional communities are merely one aspect of the New Age. There are bookstores that satisfy the appetite for "consciousness transformation," success in the marketplace, and simple spiritual formulae. These bookstores serve very much to nurture the minds of those who are convinced of the narrowness and imperialism of traditional Christianity and who wish to dabble, with a kind of "spiritual" fascination, in "other religions." "Diversity breeds relativity" is a point of view that sets aside the question of truth; sometimes it fosters naive notions that all religions lead to the same end and that one is as good or true as another.

There are workshops, gatherings, and ceremonies that people may attend, exploring among other topics the wisdom of Native American traditions or any of the transformational techniques mentioned previously. And, of course, there are the shops that channel a sense of the mysterious, of being in a world of secrets and occult powers. Symbols of yin and yang; the ancient Egyptian ankh; rock crystals; statues of Buddha, Krishna, Kali, and Ganesh; Orthodox Christian crosses and icons—all these furnishings of heterogeneous religiosity are available. Outfitted with incense and the paraphernalia of meditation, these shops are like temples of New Age adventure. Shirley MacLaine and channeling also belong to this curious new religious scene. Spangler refers to these elements as popular, glamorous, and exotic, but incidental to the intentional communities devoted to the advent of planetary culture. Yet surely the popular manifestations, undisciplined and somewhat faddish, are themselves a sign of a radical change in religious thought and practice. "Though the New Age cults have no more than about thirty thousand members," writes Harold Bloom, "their fellow travellers are an untold multitude."[8] Cult membership is only one facet of New Age religiousness.

The New Age, therefore, is expressive of plenum as well as planet. It refers to extravaganza, the superabundance of wisdom, insight, and communication that are part of the fullness of things that the planet represents. The New Age is symbolic of the effort to transform diversity into pluralism. It is certainly an expression of the acceptance of diversity as itself a transforming good, a way to express the ultimate order and meaning of existence. However, it is driven by a naive assumption that human beings act in conformity with their visions of the good. It fails to learn from the traditions themselves that the human condition is a dilemma—that, as Martin Luther affirmed, human beings are simultaneously "saints and sinners." The pluralistic acceptance of diversity must not ignore the valuable insights of the traditions that it accepts; to do so essentially amounts to a rejection of those very traditions.

Non-Organizational Organization

The idea of a "non-organizational organization" is a response to the organizational complexities and competitive diversity of the "old age." One of the axioms of modern thought has been the notion that, on the human level, anything socially intentional must be advanced by contractual association. In modern religious understanding, the church exists as the collectivity of its individual members. The church is defined, therefore, as an association of believers, an assembly or gathering. One "joins" a church;

just as readily, one quits, leaves. A prominent modern notion is that one contracts with others; contracts are "entered into" and "dissolved."

Apparently, in the minds of early Christians, there was a reality known as "Church" that made it always greater than the sum of its parts. St. Paul, therefore, referred to the Church as the "Body of Christ"; and by the second century C.E. there was consensus among Christians that to speak of God, Christ, and the Holy Spirit required comparable attention to the Church. The Apostles' Creed affirms faith in God as Creator, Christ as Redeemer, and the Holy Spirit as Sanctifier and Reconciler (in this instance affirming an organic and relational understanding of person). The Creed is structured in this fashion:

> I believe in the Holy Spirit,
> the holy catholic Church,
> the communion of saints,
> the forgiveness of sins,
> the resurrection of the body,
> and the life everlasting.

Note that "the holy catholic Church" is an affirmation of faith; it is part of the *divine context* in which all important elements of existence are understood. For the Christian, apparently, faith was an integral matter expressing a reality that is greater than the sum of its parts because it is creator, redeemer, reconciler. It was creative of a community (the holy catholic Church) that communicates our "personhood" as communion of saints (*not* communion of perfect people). It would be difficult to think of oneself as affirming, "I believe in the Holy Spirit, the holy catholic Church," if by that one meant, "I believe in this organization that I have joined, this collection of individuals that we have put together."

Traditional peoples (those untouched by some of the assumptions of modernity) have always understood this organic and holistic view of person. In December 1986, a trial lawyer by the name of S. M. Otieno died suddenly of heart failure in Nairobi, Kenya. He was a very modern person who led the life of many upper-middle-class Americans, even educating his children in the United States. Otieno had been raised as a member of an ethnic group called the Luo, a very traditional people who live about 200 miles from Nairobi. The Luos avoid modern ways entirely; they maintain traditional marriages with dowries, oppose circumcision, and believe that untraditional burial encourages evil spirits to disrupt the lives of their community.

Otieno had left the ways of his people behind him. He rarely visited them, refused to speak their language, and was married across ethnic lines to a woman of the rival Kikuyus. He had not spoken with some of his relatives for more than twenty years. Otieno thought of himself in the modern, Western sense, as an individual, not as belonging to a community, a people. His decisions and his life were his own, in his understanding. He had provided his wife with instructions for his funeral and his burial on his own land.

However, immediately after his death, Otieno's relatives sought to claim the body for the proper Luo burial. "Once a Luo, always a Luo"— the Luos feared that spirits would haunt their villages if the body were not given the proper ritual burial in their homeland. Thus began a rather bizarre battle for Otieno's corpse. The courts eventually recognized the claims of the Luos, and the decaying body was awarded to them after five months of heated argument. Of course, nothing was ultimately settled because the case is representative of the contemporary struggle between two understandings of the human person.

When New Age proponents gather in their "non-organizational communities," they are manifesting the tension between the traditional and the modern. To the traditional mind, a person is always a communal or social entity; to the modern mind, a person is *a private, individual,* entity. The modern mind tends to maintain a condescending and authoritative attitude toward the traditional mind. The former denies the latter any real share in decision making; and, indeed, it must be so if the modern agenda of manipulating nature and humanity in keeping with some grand scheme of "progress" is to succeed. However, we have seen that the "New Age" can be somewhat ambivalent. On the one hand, it projects the meaning of existence into the future, with a sense that that future has already begun to take shape; it does so with great confidence in, and loyalty to, the theories of modern science. On the other hand, it rejects the ways of the "old age," including much of modernity. This repudiation of the old age encompasses a renunciation of the organizational and institutional ways of the past. We are not talking about a "church," say the New Age apologists; we are not advocating another society for some kind of social reform. We are a new thing, a spontaneous emergence of small groups representing a new consciousness that conspires to be the soul of the planet, bringing all beings into a divine unity.

There is intention behind New Age conventicles, just as there was intention behind the conventicles and classes of eighteenth-century Pietism. It is an intention to renew, to raise consciousness, to go beyond established orders. Intention creates organization and institution; there is no avoiding it. But part of the *intention* is to avoid the stultifying feature that characterizes most institutions—the tendency to make intention and motivation subservient to organizational maintenance. Now, of course, in the past Pietist conventicles have sought to become non-organizational organizations as well. To some extent they have succeeded—they have infused established religions with a moralistic and sentimental approach that has worked toward the privatization of religion. Lutheran and Reformed Christian traditions in America, for example, have been suffused with notions of private morality and subjective experience that remove religion from the public sphere. But Pietism has also frequently led to the creation of new religious institutions that contributed to greater diversity.

There is no doubt that New Age consciousness is a response to diversity. It seeks to transcend heterogeneity and avoid its competitive and institutional disposition. But this idea of non-organizational organization contributes to the difficulty of effectively analyzing the New Age. Intentional communities have led to the founding of the New Life Foundation; the Bear Tribe Medicine Society; the Fendhorn Foundation; the Light of Christ Community Church of Tahlequah, Oklahoma; the Chinook Learning Community; Lindisfarne; and Matthew Fox's Institute in Culture and Creation Spirituality. They also have led to confusion and conflict.

Divine Immanence

A certain characteristic of New Age religiousness was already articulated by Ralph Waldo Emerson when he informed his auditors that everyone had immediate and unmediated access to the truth, beauty, and goodness of the "Over-Soul." The past was gone, according to Emerson. As William Clebsch put it in his discussion of "The Hospitable Universe of Ralph Waldo Emerson": "A new age was dawning, in which the entire inheritance of specifically religious expressions, however reformed and revitalized, would fail to evoke real reverence. In that age persons must look elsewhere than to religion for *ways to awaken and articulate their religious sentiments*" (italics mine).[9]

Although Emerson's "Over-Soul" appears to be monistic, it embraces a "dash of pluralism." The emphasis upon divine immanence is in keeping with the idea that there is no transcendence. There is only continuity in the totality of being, no discontinuity. New Age thinkers, like Emerson, may deny the charge of pantheism, but it is a curious dilemma in which they find themselves. There is no supernature, they say, no transcendence. Transcendence and immanence, natural and supernatural, are simply two words (in either case) for the same thing. If there is no discontinuity, of course, in the "experience" of reality or in the perception of it, then there are simply different modes of perceiving what is called "nature." If there is only divine immanence, only continuity in the scheme of things, then, in effect, there is no divinity at all, only the performances and rhetoric of human beings—which to some people are absurd. The point is, if it is necessary and possible to perceive the world and ourselves differently from our ordinary perception, then we are forced to admit that there is reality "other" than what we ordinarily perceive. That has led us in the past to use words like "supernatural" and "transcendent."

The New Age vision of divine immanence and unity of all being is itself one way of perceiving reality. Like Emerson, New Age proponents seek oneness and universality in the face of rampant diversity. According to this point of view, my perception of reality may be primarily concerned with the world of my people, the Luo or the Hopi, but it may also have a place for all "others" in the scheme of things. And therefore the oneness and universality of being is also an element in my perception. The New Age vision of a monistic reality wants everyone to accept the vision, to surrender to true oneness. Our importance as persons emerges from our being in touch with the oneness we share with all others. At this point the issue of diversity becomes evident because we must admit the distinctiveness of others into our personhood. When distinctiveness is heightened it requires recognition. Therein is the diversity. When New Age thought attempts to address what is really real, it affirms a monistic assumption. But when it gets down to the business of how we know what is real, it is encouraged in the direction of pluralism.

New Age religiousness emphasizes universality and monism. It does so in response to the competitive diversity of the past, a pluralism of conflict. But its own universal vision is disdainful of those who retain a more traditional view of universality and affirm a greater discontinuity in reality. The Amish, for example, maintain that the world as we perceive it exists in a fallen state. Human beings live in a state of disobedience to the created order of God's intentions. But God has provided a means to bridge the gap, through the creation of community among those who live for each other and for the earth that is our mother. Christ is the way. He is the model and the teacher; He is the Savior who helps us to overcome the discontinuity that is everywhere present. The Amish live as this community of reconciliation. They do not judge the rest of the world, but they can have little to do with it because it constantly disrupts community by its disobedience and magnification of individual self-interest. The Amish perceive the discontinuity and seek to transcend it.

The New Age consciousness accuses traditional religious communities like the Amish of advocating a notion of sin (discontinuity) that keeps human beings from affirming their oneness. Matthew Fox, a Dominican priest whose New Age proclivities have alienated him from Roman Catholicism, maintains that the Christian worldview has emphasized too much the sin and discontinuity that separate us from the divine. It would seem that a repudiation of discontinuity leads to a rejection of some people who advocate it. It would also seem that rejection of discontinuity on behalf of a monistic faith may lead to a naive conception of how the life of the planet is to be transformed.

Beyond Life and Death

If the New Age is characterized by a concern for non-organizational organizations and a devotion to universalism and monism, it is led by these
convictions into a fascination with the deathlessness of conscious energy.
On the popular level this includes interest in such occult practices as
channeling and psychic reading; on the more sophisticated level advocated by those devoted to intentional communities, it leads to assumptions about forms of human creativity that make death a matter of negative vision. According to this thinking, if we are indeed one with all that
is, then invisible elements in the scheme of things are as real as what is
visible. People begin to ask whether death is what it seems to be. They
hear that energy is not destroyed, but simply changes form. They wonder
whether this has anything to do with the stories one occasionally hears
about haunted houses and apparitions.

When my young family moved to State College, Pennsylvania, we occupied a Cape Cod house that had been previously owned by an elderly
widow who only very reluctantly gave it up. My wife and daughters
claimed that they occasionally were aware of a woman in a pale flowered
dressing gown who moved through the dining room and up the center
stairs of the house. In Tempe, Arizona, there is a restaurant that occupies
a former residence associated with an early-twentieth-century governor.
Patrons tell of seeing a woman in the costume of an earlier time behind
the bar. She disappears as readily as she appears. She has been seen de-
scending the stairs from the second floor, where the former bedrooms
now serve as small dining salons. In one of these dining areas, customers
have reported looking aside during their conversations and seeing a couple seated at the other end of the table, again in period dress.

Obviously, it is possible to advance numerous explanations for these
kinds of experiences. There are psychological theories and there are ex-
plications derived from physics and biology. The most persistent com-
ment among those skeptics among us is that people who see things have
"overactive imaginations." However, when we relegate these matters to
the imagination, we tend to admit that the imagination is something we
are not particularly fond of, something we have little experience of. It
could very well be the case that what we call "imagination" is an element
of human perception that has been dulled by the modern, technocorporate world. To the person who imagines something, the mode of thinking
and acting is affected, influenced. Something may be "more real," more
effective, wise, or useful as imagined than as bumped into by ordinary
touch, sight, or sound.

Marilyn Ferguson writes of the musings of Jeremy Bernstein, professor of
physics at Stevens Institute of Technology, who sometimes imagines that he
is an established professor at the University of Berne in 1905. He answers

his telephone and someone he has never heard of identifies himself as a patent examiner in the Swiss National Patent Office. The caller says that he understands Bernstein to be a lecturer in electromagnetic theory. "I have some ideas you might be interested in," says the voice of the patent examiner. Another crazy person with no credentials. Oh, well, what *kind* of ideas?

> He begins discussing some crazy-sounding notions about space and time. Rulers contract when they are set in motion; a clock on the equator goes at a slower rate than the identical clock placed at the North Pole; the mass of an electron increases with its velocity; whether or not two events are simultaneous depends on the frame of reference of the observer.[10]

If this had happened, what would Bernstein have done? Hung up the phone on Albert Einstein, just another person with an overactive imagination?

Perhaps the observation of the functional cessation and decay of a human body is nothing more than an imaginative failure to note the passage of personal energy. Sometimes this is realized by the popular imagination, and people begin to search for ways to perceive life on "the other side." The fact is that the planet really has begun to change radically, as the more sophisticated New Agers like Spangler and Ferguson claim. The diversification of ideas and experiences that have blossomed in the American consciousness, and in the emerging global civilization, remind us that we have developed a rather monotonous and one-dimensional way of life. The wisdom and experience of the great religious traditions may have something to teach us about death.

Buddhists, for example, inform us that we are enslaved to a very restricted notion of selfhood. We avoid developing a consciousness of death because it represents the termination of this restricted ego that lives by desire. Some Buddhist traditions require meditation on what is repulsive to the enslaved ego. One gazes, for example, at "swollen corpses, bluish corpses, festering corpses, fissured corpses, gnawed corpses, scattered corpses, hacked and scattered corpses, bloody corpses, worm-eaten corpses, and skeletons." Within medieval Benedictine monasteries skeletons and skulls were sometimes kept in secluded cells as "visual aids" to facilitate meditation upon death. Now to most of us, this kind of activity sounds morbid. But within the religious traditions using these death techniques, the goal is liberation, enlightenment. The ego that fears death is transcended and one is able to perceive "the other side."

The Tibetan Book of the Dead helps the individual prepare for death by imagining it in such a way that the journey is blissful. The devotees of New Age ideas and practices are aware of this wisdom. On the popular level they engage in channeling and shamanistic ways of realizing the community of personal energy that transcends death as we know it. Death is the great teacher. It reminds us that we must perceive things differently than

the mandates of consumerism allow, or else resign ourselves to the termi-
nation of reality seemingly symbolized by automotive graveyards. Wilfred
Smith, in *Towards a World Theology*, relates the story of Barlaam and
Josaphat, a mythic account that may be found in a variety of languages and
religious traditions. Although it appears in Christianity, Judaism, and
Islam, it probably originated in India because it parallels the story of
Gautama Buddha. Josaphat is a young Indian prince who gave up his family, his wealth, and his power in order to find an answer to the problems of
sickness, old age, and death. In the course of his search (in the Latin
Christian version) the prince meets a Christian monk by the name of
Barlaam who tells him a story. Once there was a man who fell into a well
and was clinging to two vines for all he was worth. As he hung there in
great anxiety, he noticed two mice (one black and one white) that had begun to chew on the vines above him. The man knew that before long the
vines would be cut and he would plummet to his death. End of the story.[11]

The mice are night and day, the passage of time that brings us ever
closer to death. It does no good to hang onto life. The man must let go of
the vines. The point of the story is that we must learn to let go of life as
we desire it, no longer clinging to it. The death of the self we value leads
to a new life that transcends death.

From the standpoint of our interest in pluralism, it is revealing to note
that a Sanskrit word for a deified disciple of the Buddha, "bodhisattva,"
finds its way into the Persian *Bodisaf*, thence into the Arabic *Yudasaf*, the
Greek *Loasaf*, and finally the Latin *Josaphat*. The story presents truth that is
apropos of the teachings of Christianity, Islam, Manichaeanism, and
Buddhism. But even more important to our purposes is the fact that the religious diversity of our own time makes available to us ideas about life
and death that challenge the imperialism of modern knowledge. New Age
religiousness is hospitable to those ideas that celebrate the sunrise, to the
building of a consciousness that transcends the deathly old existence. The
New Age lifts up the wisdom of the many peoples and ages of humankind
in order to affirm a new unity, a oneness and coexistence of all creatures. It
is important for New Age thinking that people recognize the necessity of
the death of the old self, the self that tries to cling to what is being chewed
off. Traditional societies in the Americas and Africa have always known
that death is only a termination of what we try to cling to, that there is a
community of being that exists beyond death as we know it.

Mind Cure

New Age religiousness is also a response to the one-dimensional understanding of health and well-being that has marked the old age. Modern
health care and medical treatment have been extremely imperialistic.

They have assumed that modern knowledge and methods are superior to whatever has existed before. The modern mind has been victimized by the often-unconscious notion that "newer is truer." The modernistic model for medicine is a technological one that operates on the principle that treatment is a matter of putting something in or taking something out. One adds a chemical and takes out (by surgery) or repairs a malfunctioning part. This follows the same principle as "fixing" a lawn mower or an automobile. The technological paradigm is based upon the assumption that a human being is a functioning mechanism that is fundamentally isolated from and superior to the rest of being and nature.

Native American medicine, on the other hand, operates with a cosmological paradigm. Disease is dis-ease—the harmony of being has been disrupted. To cure someone's illness is to find a ceremonial way of reestablishing harmony. If the individual's place in the cosmic order has been violated, then there will be no health (no wholeness) until things are put in place. It will do no good merely to "fix" or repair. The modern mind looks upon ceremony and ritual as, at worst, magical and superstitious or, at best, trifling. The traditional mind is a communal, a social, mind for which ceremony is the only appropriate integral power.

There was already a break in the armor of modernity in the nineteenth century. Even before the power of modernity had reached its zenith with modern technology, there were those who understood that health is an affair of the mind. Some of these rebels, like Phineas P. Quimby and Mary Baker Eddy, tended to absolutize the mind in such a way that the materiality of existence was denied. Christian Science and the senses were at war. "God is all, and God is good," said Eddy. "This one Mind and His individuality comprise the elements of all forms and individualities, and prophesy the nature and stature of Christ, the ideal man." But Eddy was protesting the popular, materialistic understanding of the emergent science. For her, this was neither science nor Christian. In fact, it was a scientific assumption that was grounded in earlier modern ideas of a mechanical realm of nature. "The scientific sense of Being which establishes harmony," said Eddy at the convention of the National Christian Science Association held in Chicago on June 13, 1888, "enters into no compromise with finiteness and feebleness."[12]

When the Unity School of Practical Christianity was established in 1903, Charles and Myrtle Fillmore sought to work within established churches to overturn the outmoded ways of thinking of a tired old world. The mind, said Charles Fillmore, can cure itself by imaging the perfect human body. "Waiting for death in order to get a new body is the folly of ignorance. . . . When we call ourselves fleshly, mortal, finite, we manifest bodily upon a fleshly, mortal and finite plane. We sow to the flesh, and of the flesh reap corruption."[13] And Ernest S. Holmes, founder of the Church of Religious Science, wrote that scientific mental healing is the result of clear thinking that is acted upon by "Mind." "We cannot heal successfully while we recognize sickness as a reality to the Spirit."[14]

Mind cure has been an important element in American religious life since the days of Eddy and Fillmore. Some would say that it was present in the thought of Ralph Waldo Emerson. It has always represented a countercultural point of view, something "New" that has ancient and universal roots. Mind cure has influenced the secular thought of the twentieth century, especially the corporate world, where it is thought that healthy-minded and confident employees contribute to effective, productive, and profitable enterprises. It has had its more sober and restrained influence upon holistic medicine, certain forms of psychotherapy, and the positive thinking of preachers like Norman Vincent Peale, Robert S. Schuller, and Leo Bascaglio.* And it is a significant factor in the development of New Age religiousness, especially as it seeks to draw upon the pluralistic wisdom of traditional and modern scientific knowledge on behalf of a universal consciousness.

The New Age presents a fascinating chapter in the story of religious diversity and its foreshadowing of pluralism. America is the culture of pluralism because it has been the setting for a multitude of responses to religious diversity. Most of these responses have been in deference to the need for genuine pluralism. Pluralism itself is an elusive perception of reality. It is not easy to manifest; however, American culture has been shaped by this struggle to affirm the order and meaning of diversity itself.

Notes

1. William A. Clebsch, *American Religious Thought* (Chicago: University of Chicago Press, 1973), p. xvi.

2. Marilyn Ferguson, *The Aquarian Conspiracy* (Los Angeles: J. P. Tarcher, 1980), pp. 19, 23.

3. Ibid., p. 31.

4. See H. Richard Niebuhr, *The Kingdom of God in America* (New York: Harper & Row, 1937), esp. chaps. 4, 5.

5. Catherine L. Albanese, *Nature Religion in America* (Chicago: University of Chicago Press), p. 153.

6. Richard E. Wentz, *Religion in the New World: The Shaping of Religious Traditions in the United States* (Minneapolis: Fortress Press, 1990), chap. 17.

7. Mary Farrell Bednarowsky, *New Religions: The Theological Imagination in America* (Bloomington: Indiana University Press, 1989), pp. 15–18.

*Bascaglio is not a clergyman in the traditional sense, but his lecturing is clearly influenced by the paradigm of the evangelical preacher.

8. Harold Bloom, *The American Religion* (New York: Simon & Schuster, 1992), p. 181.

9. Clebsch, p. 82.

10. Ferguson, p. 170.

11. Wilfred C. Smith, *Towards a World Theology* (Philadelphia: Westminster Press, 1981), pp. 7–11, 19–20.

12. Mary Baker Eddy, quoted in Edwin S. Gaustad, *A Documentary History of Religion in America*, vol. 2 (Grand Rapids, MI: Wm. B. Eerdmans, 1982), p. 246.

13. Charles Fillmore, quoted in Edwin S. Gaustad, *A Documentary History of Religion in America*, vol. 2 (Grand Rapids, MI: Wm. B. Eerdmans, 1982), p. 248.

14. Ernest S. Holmes, quoted in Edwin S. Gaustad, *A Documentary History of Religion in America*, vol. 2 (Grand Rapids, MI: Wm. B. Eerdmans, 1982), p. 250.

8

The Mandate of Pluralism

The culture of religious pluralism is one in which the diversity of American life is accepted and affirmed as the ultimate order and meaning of existence. Pluralism is a diversity of which Americans should become appreciatively aware; it is the religious awakening to the fundamental good of diversity.

Pluralism acknowledges diversity as a meaningful good. It is a perception of reality that accepts the significance of the diverse traditions as contributions to the well-being of humankind. Pluralism seeks to learn from traditions like secularism, Buddhism, Christianity, and Judaism; it does not exclude any of the traditions that have sought to express the ultimate order and meaning of existence. In a pluralistic culture there is no room for the secularist who does not acknowledge the richness of Christianity, just as there is no room for the Christian who is not willing to learn from the secularist.

The culture of pluralism requires the nurturing of an imagination that rationally contemplates the goodness of diversity. The culture must nurture the interrelationship of traditions, recognizing what each has to offer in our effort to live with what Reinhold Niebuhr called our "romantic over-estimate of human virtue and moral capacity."[1] "Imagination" is not an illusory, emotional, or sentimental term. It recognizes the importance of "imaging" to the intellectual, scholarly, scientific, and rational activities of human beings. Where there is no excellence in imaging, the intelligence falters and becomes captive to its own intricate calculations, fostering a world of idiot savants.

Imagining a Pluralistic America

A story. From the mad Hasid, Nahman of Bratzlav. There was once a prince who lost his mind and imagined that he was a rooster. He took off his clothes and huddled in the dining hall of the palace refusing to have anything to do with the royal fare on the table above him. All he wanted was the grain fed to the roosters. The king was beside himself. What could he do? He called in his physicians. They observed; they conferred and consulted, but they could do nothing. He sent for magicians and monks, miracle makers and holy men. All their efforts were in vain.

But one day a sage appeared who was a stranger to the royal house. "I think I can restore the mind of the prince," he said very modestly. "May I please try?"

"Of course! Please do what you can!" said the king.

Well, to the astonishment of the court, the sage took off all his clothes, huddled under the table with the prince, and began to crow like a rooster. The prince gave a suspicious frown and asked, "Who? What are you and why are you here?"

"And you?" answered the sage. "Who are you and what are you doing here?"

"That's plain for you to see. I'm a rooster, of course!"

"Ah, very interesting," replied the sage. "Curious that you should be here, too."

"What do you mean? Why curious?"

"Well, after all, it's obvious isn't it? You see? I'm a rooster, too, just like you."

And so the prince and the sage became close friends and swore always to be loyal to each other. Then one day the sage did a strange thing. He put on a shirt. "What? Are you mad?" asked the prince. "Are you trying to look like a man? Don't you remember who you are?"

"Oh, don't worry," said the sage, very matter-of-factly. "Don't ever think that a rooster who puts on a shirt stops being a rooster." It made sense. The prince agreed. And so the next day both "roosters" dressed like men. The sage grew hungry and sent for some delicacies from the royal kitchen. "What?" cried the prince, quite apprehensively. "Are you going to eat like *them*, too?" His friend said calmly, "Don't be afraid! Don't ever think that when you eat man's food at his table, you stop being a rooster. A rooster is a rooster. You shouldn't ever think that a rooster who behaves like a man becomes human. Why, you can do all the human things you want. You can live in a human world, do things for humans, and still be the same good old rooster you really are."

It made sense. The prince went back to his life as a prince.

Human beings can imagine almost anything they want to. But the imagination should never be divorced from behavior. It should never be separated from the intellect. Imagination must always help us to live with others, because what we are is always determined by what we imagine together.

We have seen, in these chapters, a great many ways in which human beings imagine their existence. In the past it was easier to imagine that you were a rooster, to keep company only with the other roosters, and to imagine that your world of roosterdom was the only world. But today that kind of imagining seems almost like madness. Madness is the inability of the individual to imagine a world that includes others.

In the culture of American pluralism, it must become possible to identify with others who are not of our tribe. It is true that the postmodern world has liberated people, permitting them to claim the richness of their traditions and the uniqueness of their identities. However, this has often led to a recurrence of the posturing found in earlier experiences of diversity. Liberated peoples begin to say, "Leave us alone; we have our own laws, our own ways; we don't want to live like you do. We are going to crawl under the table where we can live the way of the rooster. Don't ever try to come down here. We won't tell you any of the secrets of being a rooster. We don't want you to take anything that is ours. Keep away from us."

Now, it may be that those people who live in the rest of the palace are the crazy ones. Perhaps they spend too much time fussing over royal delicacies or parading around in outlandish clothes, each one trying to outdo the other. Sometimes they get into fights with each other, even kill each other. They may steal grain from the roosters or try to fatten the roosters so they can later eat them. All of this may be true. This kind of unpredictable behavior might be the reason you decided to take off those silly clothes, wear only your natural bodies, and live under the table with your own madness, away from the perceived madness of the rest of the palace. But, of course, we are not roosters, and it would be difficult to live in the palace without relating to the other creatures who live there. The table is *in* the palace.

The New Tribalism

Recently I participated in a national dialogue on "Immigrant Culture, Values, and Identity," sponsored by the Arizona Humanities Council and the National Endowment for the Humanities. The dialogue sessions were held at various sites in Arizona, and culminated in a televised conversation broadcast from several locations simultaneously. A Navajo woman from Tuba City spoke of a white Christian culture that tries to make everyone act the same and that has no respect for other cultures. "We have our own laws, our own ways, on the reservation," she said. "We want to live that way, and leave it at that." A mediator in Tucson, at the end of the session, identified himself as a "tribal person." "When I hear all this talk about democracy," he said, "I get uneasy. I feel it somehow invades my tribal world. You know, I think the future is going to be tribal."

As we imagine a pluralistic America, we must affirm the rights and the values of "tribal" existence. People are fearful of the juggernaut. They see the rich diversity and the particularities of history, of personality and peoplehood, being threatened by the onslaught of some kind of imperialistic conformity. They want to preserve uniqueness, special meaning, and identity. They want to know who they are in the plot of a meaningful story that provides order for existence. The "tribal" mind is a communal mind. There is an uneasiness about democracy, because that has come to mean the right of all to do as they please and think as they please. The kind of individualism that has been fostered in the American republic breeds fragmentation, discord, and wastefulness that can only be controlled by collective institutions continually feeding the selfish hunger to consume.

I imagine a tribal America in which distinctiveness is allowed to exist, and not just as a novelty to be enjoyed by tourists who want to see "others" in their traditional costumes, engaged in curious occupations. I imagine a tribal America also because I hope that a new sense of community will replace America's myopic individualism. A restoration of tribal values would re-create a world in which the individual existed as part of and *for* the community, rather than one in which the community existed as a collective association of individuals. In a tribal society there are no garish celebrities because there is no need for them; celebrities can never emerge in tribal society because they destroy community.

However, I imagine a tribalism that will be altogether new. Americans will be very much aware of "many tribes." The old tribalism was often the basis for considerable conflict and bloodshed. Jacinto, in Willa Cather's *Death Comes for the Archbishop*, explains to Bishop Latour the reasons why the Ácoma people built their village upon a naked rock. "A man can do a whole lot," he says, "when they hunt him day and night like an animal. Navajos on the north, Apaches on the south; the Ácoma run up a rock to be safe." Cather goes on to tell her readers:

> All this plain, the Bishop gathered, had once been the scene of a periodic manhunt; these Indians, born in fear and dying by violence for generations, had at last taken this leap away from the earth, and on that rock had found the hope of all suffering and tormented creatures—safety. They came down to the plain to hunt and to grow their crops, but there was always a place to go back to. If a band of Navajos were on the Ácoma's trail, there was still one hope; if he could reach his rock—Sanctuary! On the winding stone stairway up the cliff, a handful of men could keep off a multitude. The rock of Ácoma had never been taken by a foe but once, —by Spaniards in armour.[2]

It was not easy for tribes to compete with each other for the right to sacred lands and the sacred creatures who offered themselves as food. The old tribalism relied to a great extent upon a very protracted mobility. It took considerable time to traverse the mountains, deserts, plains, and rivers that separated tribes. There was no easy communication to provide instantaneous conversation or information over great distances. It is not likely, short of a holocaust or natural catastrophe, that we shall soon have the opportunity to begin the evolution of human society over again, by some miraculous return to the tribal life of the ancient Americas. And so, if the future we imagine is to be tribal, it will be a new tribalism.

Native Americans, like all human beings, must remember that they are aware of their tribalism because there is another world that signified them, with which they must reckon. There are many tribes; and, in a world of rapid transport and easy communication, we cannot avoid each other. There must be laws that address this larger world of new tribalism as well as the laws of individual tribes. The new tribalism cannot exist as a laissez-faire dispersion of peoples, each with its own mountain or river. It is a kind of madness to think so—a kind of "roosterism." The table is *in the palace*, where there are humans who do not act like roosters act. The Pan-Indianism of North America is itself a creation of the new tribalism, the emergence of a new consciousness that is shared by those who know the beauty of the tribal way and who have suffered at the hands of those who would crush all tribes for the sake of progress or salvation. Even the awareness of the value of one's tribal existence takes place in relation to a world "out there"—in the palace.

Respect as a Mark of Acceptance

The new tribalism is an act of imagination. To accept diversity and transform it into pluralism is to learn to respect the others who reside in the place with us. Respect is a mark of our ability to observe "others" as part of the multiplicity of our own selfhood. To imagine the new tribalism is to recognize that the order and meaning of existence are known communally. The community, the people, are primary. Modern democracy asserts the primacy of the individual. A basic precept at work among traditional peoples is respect, the quality of understanding oneself in relation to others. The driver of an automobile in contemporary American society is an encapsulated ego. The car is hers; she is in control. She drives as fast as she pleases. She passes through intersections without regard for the changing light or the other drivers who have been waiting for the opportunity to do the same. Respect is not a quality that is easily learned; it is a derivative attribute—attributed to the people to whom one belongs. Respect is a way of recognizing that my own selfhood is bound up with the selfhood of others. I am not a private ego; I *am* my brothers and sisters. Respect always thinks for and on behalf of the "others," whether the other is human, animal, or vegetable; whether the clouds in the sky, the rocks in the field, or the waters of the stream. If it is the "other" who is disrespectful of the grass, the deer, or the oncoming driver, he must still be respected. I must think for him and with him because he has lost his sense of belonging, or perhaps his people never taught it to him to begin with.

Reverence as a Mark of Acceptance

To accept diversity is to learn to imagine our respect as a measure of the mystery resident in all relationships. Respect is extended into reverence.

We must learn to revere the "others," to deepen our respect to the point of honor and caring. Our reverence is not only for those who are like us or think as we do; it is not only for humans or even for all sentient beings; it is for *all* of being. We must imagine respect and reverence for all of being. We can derive this imagination from those whose tribal understanding has already known it. In the new pluralism we are not left to ourselves and our own resources. Some traditional peoples may be reluctant to share their deepest wisdom, because modern American culture has taken from them without asking and without reciprocating. And so they try to retain the secrets of their traditions. But they cannot long remain secret in this world of global diversity. There are many who will distort those secrets if the traditional peoples do not agree to become their teachers. Pluralism demands risks from all of us. As we learn reverence and respect, we will also become humble enough to allow ourselves to be taught. We will always *give* when we take or receive. The new tribalism will teach us the communal character of existence and may enable us to overcome the fragmentary individualism of the modern world.

Now, of course, traditional peoples are not collectives of perfect individuals. Sometimes they act as if they were the most important element in the fullness of being. They lose their respect and reverence for the earth. They do not take care of things as they should. They want what the people of the outside, consumerist, society have; and they will do anything to get those "things." Sometimes there are individuals in the traditional community who lose touch with their people, their ways. In traditional understanding, the only means of restoring the health of the community or the individual is ceremony. Ceremony is beyond ordinary rationality, beyond morality. Ceremony is the action of communal memory that imagines the wholeness of being when people disrupt the ultimate order and meaning of things. The new tribalism can help us to rediscover ceremony, the only act of human imagination that puts together what is broken, what is beyond our technical reason to fix, or beyond our moral will to correct. Ceremony may be the most sophisticated utilization of the human mind. It represents the human imagination at its most creative; it is an aspect of our humanity that was taken from us by the imperialism of technical reason in the modern world. Ceremony enacts unity where there is only disorder and fragmentation.

Refinement: A Mark of Acceptance

I frequently tell my students that if they leave the university having undergone no transformation in their taste, their behavior, their language, then they have not been educated and their professors have failed them. Refinement imagines the kind of existence in which respect and reverence

have exalted the human enterprise and lifted that enterprise to a new order of beauty and harmony. When I tell my students about refinement,
they frown and look at each other quizzically. They have never given any
thought to making changes in what they like and how they speak. Their
"education" involves the acquisition of information and the accumula-
tion of "credits." But refinement is a quality of existence that applies to
people of all tribes, religions, and cultures. It is basically a question of
what we consider to be the best exemplification of our people, our way of
life. When the tribe is at its best there is harmony; and harmony is beauty.
The crudities of existence have been polished, refined, made useful by the
respect and reverence that are part of the community. Refinement is the
imagination of the "more than," a recognition that our lives are more than
we have yet made of them. As we live among each other in the culture of
pluralism, we must imagine what it is that we can receive from others,
and what it is that we can give to others in respect and reverence. The
"other" is as much an element in our refinement as are the teachings and
habits of our own people. An honest and civil attempt to respect the
"other" will lead to an awareness of what may contribute to the refinement of our own ways.

Refinement asks that we behave in certain ways only because "our people" have always acted in this way or because our encounters with new
peoples demand it. Manners are an aspect of refinement. Oftentimes
manners in and of themselves make no sense. Also, we live in a period in
which manners are declining, partly as a result of the Christian era's
demise. The Christian era was a cultural period in which the integrity of
society was maintained by certain "habits of the heart"—forms of behavior that just *belonged* without requiring constant deliberation. Now, however, habits that were instilled in me as a child are no longer considered
essential. They are thought to be naive or silly, perhaps even irrational. In
my childhood these habits were maintained by parents, grandparents,
uncles, aunts, school, and church. They were simply part of how one be-
haved. Either "our people" did it this way, or "that's just the way you act
in polite society." Manners are not utilitarian or functional; they are not
necessary to physical survival. But they are necessary to the refinement of
the human venture. They are the mark of community. When I open the
door for a woman or for an elder, I am not suggesting that either is inferior or helpless. I am expressing an order and refinement to living that is
not based upon my egocentric needs *or* those of the woman or elder.
Rather, it is a measure of harmony and beauty that recognizes the inter-
dependence of existence.

Women used to wear hats in public and at church services. Men removed their hats indoors, and in the presence of God or a woman. On the
surface, there seems to be no reason for these habits. However, their real

value to modern society is in the aesthetics of living and as a measure of the fact that we are a people who do things this way. The decline in manners is an indication that society has no deference to others, no respect for the community. The decline in manners occurs in the absence of community and in the ascendancy of the illusory private individual "who does as he damned well pleases." He plays his music in defiance of all others. He does not think of what kind of neighbor he is being. He lives as an atomized entity, which is a state demonstrably more destructive to human existence than to atoms.

Civility and Peace: Too Many Voices?

In an interview about his novel *In the Beauty of the Lilies,* John Updike raises the question, "What do we take forward as a species into the 21st century? How much will be left of what we think of as human?" In the novel, Updike introduces his readers to the lives of several generations of the Wilmot family, beginning in 1910 with Clarence, a Presbyterian minister in Paterson, New Jersey, who undergoes a crisis of faith and loses all sense of the meaning of existence. As George Steiner put it in an article about the novel:

> Clarence, the lapsed man of the cloth, begets Teddy, who carries the mail and begets Esther, who changes her name, rises to glamour, and begets deranged Clark, whom the flames consume in expiation to a nonexistent but vengeful Moloch. . . . History unfolds richly in the background. Currier & Ives will yield to CNN. Distant World Wars, the Depression, the drama of a Lindbergh or a New Deal impinge, sometimes heavily, on the works and days of Paterson. . . . There is a new weekly, *The New Yorker,* whose cover "had a chalky drawing of white-faced shoppers walking at night . . . past a store window holding a Christmas tree and a hollow-eyed, sinister Santa Claus."[3]

Updike is portraying the thingification of human existence as an all-consuming world that breeds intolerance of any other reality. In his interview with Joan Connell of the Religion News Service, Updike speaks of popular culture, of what it reveals of the dramatic changes that have taken place. What we used to get from the movies was "two hours of release from the burdens of the real world . . . you got role models, you got examples of grace—human grace—Fred Astaire's grace, Gary Cooper's grace, the grace of all those heroines."[4] According to Updike, the old studio moguls gave us a fun world in which virtue was rewarded and vice punished. There was a kind of happiness and direction to it all. "You go to the movies now and feel you've witnessed a kind of mess. There are too many voices, too many attempts to please this or that segment of the imagined audience. There's no real aesthetic, no sense of anybody being in charge. There are too many people trying to inform us, there is a terrible lack of peace."[5]

Updike's novel well portrays the crisis in the diversity of the American culture of religious pluralism. He points out the danger of "too many voices, too many attempts to please . . . too many people trying to inform." It is difficult to find civility, to imagine a peace, a commonality, a unity that would facilitate the move from rampant diversity to a culture of pluralism. The old movies portrayed a rigorous moral order, an aesthetic, a happiness that gave a sense of well-being to people who know that they exist in a state of suspension between their faith in the "more than" and the ironic circumstances of everyday life.

Into the Depth of Tradition

Two things must happen. We must descend into the powerful and nurturing depths of our own religious traditions, and we must accept and extend ourselves into the traditions of others. The religious traditions of human history are not the optional artifacts we make them out to be in this secular and consumerist society. Religious traditions have everything to do with who we are, who we have been, and the ways in which we have given order and meaning to existence. In the twentieth-century society portrayed by Updike, Americans assume that religious traditions are optional interests that can be ignored or rejected. Many people, like Clarence Wilmot, have experienced a crisis of faith or an alienation from religious institutions, practices, and people that has been stultifying and disillusioning. Their response has often been one of total rejection of all religion. However, religious traditions are greater than our experience or practice of them, more meaningful than their institutional manifestations. They are our roots; and they are a resource for managing encounters with and responses to any intellectual and ethical situation imaginable. Somewhere, sometime, someone in the tradition "has been there." Tradition is a teacher, a guide, a companion to the human pilgrimage. For this reason, the scientist, the philosopher, the secularist, the atheist, the naturalist, and the humanist must all descend into the *depths* of the religious traditions that have fashioned their world, our culture. Even the departures of modernity from those traditions and institutions have been shaped by reaction to them. And the departures have frequently been dishonest. They have not responded to religious resources at their depths; they have not encountered the best, the richest, of traditional assets.

The Hindu yogas, the Vedas, the Upanishads, the Bhagavad Gita—these are fundamental elements of human history. They will not go away; they are "once for all"; they will never be superseded. The Buddha, the Christ, the Torah, the Qur'an—they are with us always. Each represents a profound insight about the nature of reality, the human condition, and the meaning of existence. They are incarnations, embodiments of truth; from the human perspective they embody some of the noblest aspirations, some of the supreme fictions and visions of the whole and the holy. Religious traditions preserve and bear witness to these incarnations on a sophisticated level as well as on a popular level. Each tradition is both exoteric and esoteric. Each contains a level of truth that is entirely public, accessible to all people, both inside and outside the communities that preserve the tradition: That is the exoteric dimension. However, there is also the esoteric dimension that is available in steps and stages to those who are serious in their pursuit of truth and meaning, who wish to perceive reality with greater than ordinary understanding. There are secrets available only to those who are prepared to adopt a more rigorous approach. Accordingly, each tradition provides a way for the masses and a way for the questioners, the disciples.

The enlightenment represented by the Buddha provides a path for the folk who are immersed in the toil, struggle, and suffering of the quotidian. They make their offerings, say their prayers, and think that the Buddha shares his enlightenment with them. But there is a level of Buddhist philosophy and discipleship attainable through monastic orders, pilgrimages, ascetic practices, and meditational techniques that provides the means for a dedicated initiate to become Buddha.

For average American Christians, Christ is Jesus, their friend and companion who lives and represents their ideals or their Savior who offers salvation to all individuals who know that He died for their sins. But there is also the Christ of St. Paul, of St. Symeon the New Theologian, of Gregory of Nyssa, or of Meister Eckhart. To the intellectual or the initiate, Christ is a new creation who is shared with the world. Christ is an irreversible event that demonstrates the cost of human willfulness and the power of God to overcome it. The Torah provides the principles, the laws by which a special nation honors the Creator and lives as the Creator wishes. The Torah is a keeping of Shabbat, a remembering of the history of God's people. But to the initiate, the Torah becomes the very essence of Creator and Creation, the reality that calls life into being and provides for its continued existence. The Torah is a perception of reality that is beyond the keeping of the Law even though it is present in that Law and its keeping.

We ignore the exoteric and esoteric levels of the great religious traditions to our own detriment. They have much to teach us. If I have been part of a family or a people that is Jewish, but I turn my back on what my Jewishness means, I will never understand myself or the world in which I live. I had best return to my teacher and learn what my religion's wisdom and practices can teach me. I cannot with integrity respond to other people unless I know my own people *at their best*. The development of the culture of pluralism requires this of us as we struggle with our diversity. There can hardly be respect, reverence, and refinement unless they arise from the depths of the traditions that have fashioned us. However, out of these depths will emerge an appreciative awareness of *others* who also have sounded the depths of *their* traditions. It is at this level that creative encounter occurs; it is here that we begin to learn from each other and from each other's traditions.

The superabundance of the culture of pluralism requires a sense of balance. Otherwise, there will continue to be chaos, fragmentation, and conflict. Otherwise, diversity represents only what Updike referred to as the culture of "too many voices, too many attempts to please this or that segment of the imagined audience . . . [a culture with] no real aesthetic, no sense of anybody being in charge . . . too many people trying to inform us." The culture of "too many voices" is a superficial culture. In the midst of this superabundance, there must be people who know who they are, people who face outward from the tradition of their roots, looking at others honestly, with reverence, respect, and refinement. Therein is the balance, the way in which we develop a state of mind that is instinctively defensive of diversity.

Notes

1. Reinhold Niebuhr, *Moral Man and Immoral Society* (New York: Charles Scribner's Sons, 1960), p. xx.

2. Willa Cather, *Death Comes for the Archbishop* (New York: Vintage Books, 1990), p. 97.

3. George Steiner, "The Supreme Fiction," *The New Yorker*, 106.

4. John Updike, interview by Joan Connell. This newspaper interview appeared after the publication of Updike's *In the Beauty of the Lilies*. The source has been misplaced.

5. Ibid.

About the Book
and Author

Religious pluralism has been a defining characteristic of the American experience since colonial times. In the twentieth century, as American society has become more radically pluralistic, the issue of religious identity has once again become prominent.

Providing a historical context, Richard Wentz examines the challenges that pluralism presents to denominationalism and civil religion and considers the contributions secularism and the New Age movement have made to the culture of religious pluralism. Finally, Wentz calls for a new pluralism based on civility and respect, a reimmersion into our religious traditions, and an extension of ourselves into the traditions of others.

Richard E. Wentz is professor of religious studies at Arizona State University.

Index